Mary Greene Chandler Ware

Death and Life

Mary Greene Chandler Ware

Death and Life

ISBN/EAN: 9783337389260

Printed in Europe, USA, Canada, Australia, Japan

Cover: Foto ©Lupo / pixelio.de

More available books at **www.hansebooks.com**

DEATH AND LIFE.

DEATH AND LIFE.

BY

MARY G. WARE,

AUTHOR OF "ELEMENTS OF CHARACTER," AND "THOUGHTS IN MY GARDEN."

TO

THE ARMY OF MOURNERS,

WHOSE TEARS ARE THE PRICE OF OUR NATIONAL EXISTENCE,

This Volume is Dedicated,

IN THE HOPE THAT IT MAY TEND TO SOFTEN THE SORROW
THAT HAS COME FROM DEATH
BY QUICKENING THEM TO A TRUER LIFE.

CONTENTS.

	PAGE
DEATH AND LIFE	9
MOURNING FOR THE DEAD	31
MEMORY IN THE FUTURE LIFE	53
SPIRITUALISM	73
THE BUILDING-UP OF REGENERATE LIFE	99
THE PAST AND THE FUTURE	133
WAR AND PEACE	157

DEATH AND LIFE.

Death is the ending of an old state, and the beginning of a new one. Every night we die as to all that concerns to-day, and every morning our awaking is a true resurrection as to all that concerns to-morrow. Each new day or state is built up out of all the preceding ones: and death is not so much *d*estruction as *c*onstruction; not a ceasing to live, but the beginning of a more advanced life.

DEATH AND LIFE.

WHOEVER contemplates life with thoughtful faith must feel convinced that God and man look upon it from a totally different point of view, and value it in an entirely different way. To most persons, life, as a mere present enjoyment, is of priceless worth, loved for its own value with a blind passion, in spite of poverty, sickness, misfortune, or bereavement. "All that a man hath will he give for his life;" and, to many, the saddest thing in life is the conviction, that it cannot in this world, with all its sorrows and its vicissitudes, continue for ever.

That uninterrupted life in this world could not be the blessing it seems is proved by the simple fact, that death is inevitable to all; that it comes oftener to the very young than to those who have reached adult life; that it interrupts us in plans and pursuits that seem to us of immense importance, cutting us down in the prime of our strength, and taking from the world those who are in the fulness of usefulness, as often as those who only cumber society with their imbecility or offend it with their wickedness.

This love of life, which is so universal and so strong as to be an instinct rather than a mere passion, is one of the attributes of man, given to him by the Creator with life itself, and must therefore be good. Why, then, does the Creator disappoint this love by what man calls premature death? Why does he so often take away life from the happy and the virtuous in their youth, and so often suffer the wretched and the wicked to live on to extreme old age? Or why, in truth, does he suffer us to die at all?

This brings us to the consideration of the great delusion under which mankind have suffered and groaned these many centuries, giving a reality, and a power not its own, to what is in truth, in great measure, a phantom of the imagination. Man weeps at death as the extinction of life, while to the Creator it is the unfolding of a higher life. The little inmates of an infant-school, full of the enjoyment of its lively amusements and employments, would be troubled, if they were told every day, that, in a short time, they would be taken away from all these pleasures. The boy with his top and marbles and story-books thinks with pain of the time when he must give them up for more serious occupations. The girl with her dolls and her baby-house finds her cup of happiness full, and wishes she might live so always. As the mind expands from year to year, it asks for maturer enjoyments and wider fields of action; and, in each step onward in life's progress, the mind, as it reaches forward to what lies before, quits its grasp on something that it leaves behind. Herein is something analogous to what we call death. As fast as the mind opens to the new, it closes to the old: it becomes alive to something it was unconscious of before; and dies to something, that, because it is outgrown, is now useless and uninteresting.

There are persons who mourn over the pleasures of the past, and who look upon childhood as the happiest period of life; but such persons are apt to be those who have made little moral progress, and who form but a feeble estimate of the value and object of their existence. It is to be hoped that the number is small of those who could be content with life without growth.

When we read of the fearful plague that befell the Egyptians; the death, in one night, of every first-born son throughout the kingdom, — it seems like something so remote from all our own experience, we cannot fully realize that a nation was ever so afflicted. Probably no people ever existed so little capable as our own of even sympathizing with such a calamity; for long-continued peace and prosperity have incapacitated us from appreciating the sufferings of less-favored races. Hitherto, death has come to us in its more gentle forms. Pestilence has been scarcely known, and violence has been still more rare. Now all is changed, and our young men are perishing daily by wounds, and by the pestilences of the camp, till we are almost like the Egyptians, with a corpse at every hearth-stone.

As death has been known to us heretofore, we have been measurably able to look upon it as a visitation of Providence: but when men are mowed down in battle; when our friend is at one moment full of life and strength, and, the next, stretched a helpless clod, felled down by the wrath of man, — we find it difficult to believe that Providence has dealt the blow. Still we know that he could have prevented it: therefore it must have fallen by his permission.

How shall we reconcile all this carnage, permitted by our heavenly Father, with our preconceived ideas of his paternal love? Some way must be found, or there is danger that our faith may be shipwrecked in the billows of our despair.

Death has for ages reigned on earth as king of terrors. The skull and cross-bones, ghastly insignia of his power, are as familiar to every eye as the crown and sceptre of earthly monarchs. The kingdom of Christ has been proclaimed eighteen hundred years, with its assurance of eternal life: but the blind eyes of mankind have failed to open to its meaning; the captives to the bondage of fear have been unable to comprehend the liberty freely offered to their acceptance. If the kingdom of Christ had come in its power into the hearts of mankind, the terrible king would have been dethroned long ago, and his crown and sceptre shattered, and crumbled into dust.

To those who live in the bondage of this fear, death seems the end of life. So shadowy and obscure to them is all beyond the grave, that it has no definite existence to their minds: and imagination shapes only phantoms, instead of men and women; and locality, without form, in place of the fair fields of earth. Yet, in reality, death is but a single point in life; and that part of life which is beyond death is incomparably more vivid, more varied, more full of interest, than that which is now around us.

We often hear the wish expressed, that life might be repeated in this world, with the aid of all the wisdom that has been gathered in its first experience. This is an unwise wish, whatever may have been the character of the life already passed. If the soul desires, from a sincere love of goodness, to lead a second life better than the first, this is exactly what death will enable it to do, with more of help and less of hinderance than it has enjoyed or suffered here, and with all the benefit of whatever wisdom it may have attained on earth. If, on the other hand, the soul only dreads to leave this world through fear of suffering in the other the results of an evil life, there is no probability that a second trial would have any other effect than to sink it into a still deeper abyss of sin.

A true faith in the providence of God teaches us, that the time selected for death is that which is best adapted to our own progress in life. We, as it were, graduate from this world, when we arrive at such a state that our future progress will go on more favorably in the spiritual world than here.

One of the principal distinctions between the temporal and the eternal world is, that here all classes of good and evil are mixed together heterogeneously, and incentives to goodness and temptations to evil are both exerting their power upon us at every step. This is allowed because the end of life here is for us to choose, in perfect freedom, between good and evil; which we could not do, unless exposed alike to both influences. In the eternal world, we are classed according to our characters,—like loving and seeking like; so that the good are delivered from the snares of the evil, and the evil from the annoyance of the good: for each are mutually distasteful to the other. In this state, the progress of the good must be far more rapid and more agreeable, because all surrounding influences are in harmony with their desires; and their temptations are those only that are in their own hearts.

Death, the passing from the present life of probation and preparation to the future life of retribution and fruition, is a subject demanding the utmost seriousness of thought; but there is no just reason for looking upon it with sadness, in relation either to ourselves or our friends. It is impossible to believe heartily in the paternal love of the Almighty, and not to believe with the apostle, that "to die is gain." Every day in the year, an army of human beings passes from the face of the earth to be swallowed up in eternity; or, let us rather say, to be clasped more closely than before in the arms of Eternal Love. Surely we cannot believe that these conscripts are taken by chance, or by the divine displeasure. If God is love, they are taken because he wishes to do that which is best for them. The world has ceased to be their true home; and it is time that they should take their places in the eternal mansions.

It is impossible for the finite mind to comprehend the Divine Providence that overrules the disposal of the lives of men. Death often seems to us to come prematurely, when a person is removed from earth whose talents promised a useful or brilliant career, or who is cut short in the midst of such a career. But the societies of heaven stand in equal need of wisdom and the power of usefulness; and the capacities that had not completed the task that seemed waiting for them here will find ample and endless scope in the regions of the future life.

There is a sadness attached to all gifts and endowments when looked upon in relation to this world only, because we know that they must grow dim and pass away : but, in the spiritual world, there is no dimness nor death but that which is the result of sin ; and all that is heavenly there becomes brighter and more perfect through the eternal ages. No soul will be there misplaced, no faculty unemployed ; and the growth in knowledge and in wisdom will know no end. In those wider fields of activity and of progress, the soul must find continual cause for rejoicing, and must look back to the hinderances, and the imperfect freedom of this life, as to a state of childhood, to which it feels no inclination to return.

The freedom of the future life is a blessing of much interest and value. In this world we are hedged about by circumstances, in a way that hinders us from doing as we would. Our social position, our opportunities of culture, our physical health, and many other limitations, press upon us, and often infringe upon our liberty. We may be free in thought and feeling in this world ; but, in the external manifestations of thought and feeling, few persons possess a freedom that is any thing more than nominal.

Swedenborg tells us, that the heavenly Father guards our internal freedom with great care, because we are responsible only so far as we are free. Whoever examines his own mind with fairness must be compelled to acknowledge, that his thoughts and feelings are free; that he is at liberty to love or hate, and to hold any form of opinion, precisely as seems to him good. The expression of his loves and hates, and of his opinions, is a different thing; because, if they are unlike those of his associates, he may have a thousand motives for concealing them, and even for assuming to hold very different ones from those which are really his. Hence come many varieties, more or less culpable, of concealment, subterfuge, insincerity, and hypocrisy.

The bondage of voluntary sin we are all able to avoid, if we will: but living in social and family relations with those who differ from us so much that we can only live in peace by often practising silence when we would gladly speak, and by many forms of external compliance that annoy and trouble us, is a bondage from which no one can escape entirely; which presses on many painfully, and on some so as to make life itself a weariness, or even an almost insupportable burden.

The "many mansions" of the future life remove from us all these sources of annoyance and trouble, and give us the truest freedom. Classed as society is there, by like seeking and joining itself to like, family and social sympathy become the rule, instead of the exception; and each one is helped on in the way he would go, by the support that sympathy gives.

Heaven is a world of sincerity, where love to the Lord and to the neighbor are the dominant impulses of every soul. In such a home, there can be no fear but that of doing wrong; and this is the liberty wherewith the Lord makes his children free.

In heaven, all are not equally sincere, nor do all equally love the Lord and the neighbor; but no one can find a place there, unless the love of truth and the desire of goodness underlie the other loves and desires of his heart.

It has been a question in many minds, how the good and the evil can be separated with justice into the two regions of heaven and hell; because it has seemed to them, that in classing the human race, although it would be very easy to place the very good and the very wicked in their appropriate homes, those who were less marked in character could hardly deserve heaven or hell; and, when it came to those who were least good and least evil, the difference between the two would be almost nothing, while the difference in their destinies would be infinite. The difference that separates the good from the evil is something much more positive than persons who reason in this way suppose. In the good, the love of the Lord and the neighbor predominates over the love of self and of the world; while, in the evil, the opposite is the case. Although the difference in external life, between many of these two classes, may be quite inappreciable to human observation, they are, in fact, walking away from each other, and their paths can never cross or approach each other. To the omniscient Eye this is at once apparent, and judgment belongs to the omniscient Mind alone. The justice of this judgment is made apparent to all, in the future life, because all are there left in freedom to choose their final abode.

When the soul quits its material body, it enters the world of spirits, which is a region between heaven and hell. It is there received kindly by good spirits, who, by their sympathy and instruction, endeavor to place the new-comer at ease, and to attract him into the society of other good spirits. If his dominant loves are good, he remains with the good spirits, and is gradually prepared to enter heaven: if his desires are bad, or if they are less advanced in goodness than those of the spirits with whom he is first placed, he turns away from them, and others of a lower order present themselves. This continues until he finds himself with those who are agreeable to him. If he prefers the society of the evil, he joins himself to them; and, as soon as he has made his choice, he passes of his own accord to the mansions appropriate to his own loves and desires. There is no external compulsion in all this, but simply a free expression, in outward act, of the principles which govern the internal life.

The mansions of the spiritual world are manifold as the minds of the spirits who dwell in them. In this world our homes represent, in some degree, the minds of those who dwell in them; but this resemblance is, with most persons, limited in various ways by external hindcrances. In the spiritual world, the external corresponds spontaneously with the internal. Not only the countenance and the person, but the dress, the house, and the garden, are the exponents of the soul that possesses them; and, as the soul changes from period to period, the things that surround it change also. Thus sincerity is the law, not only of the human soul in the spiritual world, but of that world itself. To complete the heavenly harmony, the occupations of the future life are adapted, with multifarious variety, to the capacities and talents of every soul; and each is appointed to perform the work for which he is best fitted.

Happiness or misery is thus, simply, the direct consequence of the goodness or the wickedness of the soul, and not the arbitrary reward or punishment awarded by the Almighty. He does not desire the misery of any living creature, and permits all to be as happy as they are capable of being, and to be as free as they can be, without doing harm to themselves or others. The liberty of no one is restrained in doing good; but they who would do evil to those who are about them are restrained.

It has been stated above, that all may avoid, if they will, the bondage of voluntary sin in this world; but, in the most degraded classes of society, there is a great deal of what seems to be sin incurred by those who have not liberty of choice. Little children are corrupted by wicked parents, and educated to habitual evil; and, having no knowledge of God or of religion, they are unconscious of their own immorality. Under such circumstances, human beings are not responsible; and their evil deeds are not attributed to them as sins, any more than good deeds would be attributed to them for righteousness, when done only by compulsion. It is that only which we assume from voluntary choice, whether good or evil, that is truly ours. It is easy to perceive the futility of a life of merely external, formal goodness; and a little reflection will enable us to perceive, that a life of merely external, formal wickedness is just as futile. Such goodness does the soul no good, and such wickedness does the soul no harm. They are both as external to the soul as the clothes are to the body.

When a human being who has lived a life of involuntary sin passes into the other life, he is like a new-born child. His spiritual capacities have never been opened on earth; and he wakes as from a long animal sleep, and becomes a spiritual being. Good angels minister to his ignorance, and he then first begins to be an accountable being; because he is then, for the first time, free to choose between good and evil.

Thus, with the Almighty, justice and mercy are one. No exercise of arbitrary power drives from his presence any soul that desires to remain near to him; and no soul is made incapable of this de-desire through any influence of circumstance beyond its own control. His power is equalled by his love, and seeks to make itself known and felt by the perpetual exercise of love. The salvation of the souls he has created is the whole end and aim of his providence in this world and in the next. It is God who worketh within us, both to will and to do of his good pleasure, when we strive, with fear and trembling, to work out our own salvation.

In the Scriptures, the terms " salvation " and " condemnation " are used as synonymous with life and death. To live is to be with God; to die is to be separated from him. Such life is called the kingdom of heaven, and is typified by various figures, in the teachings of the Lord to his disciples. It is the pearl of great price, the treasure hid in a field, the one thing needful. It is something so valuable, that we are wise to sell all that we have in order to obtain it. There is no danger that we shall love that life too well; and, the more we love it, the less we shall fear the death of the material body. It is but a small thing to part with life in this world, if we have the assurance of unending life in the world to come.

Everlasting life is what mankind desire above all else, — desire with fear and trembling; and there is nothing that can be looked forward to which is so terrible as everlasting death. How shall we obtain the one, and how escape from the other?

The Lord tells us, "Verily, verily, I say unto you, He that heareth my word, and believeth on Him that sent me, hath everlasting life, and shall not come into condemnation, but is passed from death unto life." And again he says, "He that believeth on the Son hath everlasting life, and he that believeth not the Son shall not see life."

The promise, it should be observed, is not of something beyond the grave, but now, in the world of time and space. He that believeth is not to have eternal life by and by in a future state, but hath it here and now. For him material death has no terror, and to him spiritual death cannot come. What, then, is that saving belief so important for us all?

To believe in the Son, and on Him who sent him, is to feel that he is the one perfect realization and source of all goodness and all truth; to feel that his love for us is such, that we must love him in return; and that the only way in which we can testify our love for him is by loving our neighbor as ourselves. These two great commandments comprise the whole law of eternal life, covering the whole ground of piety and morality, faith and works.

This is something very easy to say, but very difficult to attain; for we must sell all that we have, before we can begin to lay up treasure in heaven. Many live lives of external goodness like the young man in the Gospel; but, like him, are full of the complacency of spiritual pride, trusting that their vast possessions of good works will suffice to pay for the pearl of great price. When the truth is presented to their minds, that all goodness belongs to God, and that they must give up all trust in their own goodness if they would attain to eternal life, they are filled with disappointment and sorrow. Then they perceive the force of the Lord's words: "It is easier for a camel to go through the eye of a needle than for a rich man to enter into the kingdom of God." Nothing can indeed be more impossible than for the human soul to become regenerate, so long as it trusts in the riches of its own good works. God alone has strength to lift us out of this falsehood; and he can do it, only when we cease to trust in ourselves, and, humbling ourselves before him, confide in the saving power of his wisdom and his love.

MOURNING FOR THE DEAD.

THE creature could never lament the dispensations of the Creator, if he understood them: therefore the measure of our grief is also the measure of our ignorance.

MOURNING FOR THE DEAD.

HOW shall we mourn for the dead? Shall we mourn as if they had indeed ceased to live, or as if they had passed on before us into a higher and more perfected life? Shall we, like unbelieving Jews, roll great stones upon the graves of our friends, as if we dreaded lest perchance their bodies might escape from earth? And shall we weep over those stones, as if they indeed imprisoned all that remained to us of our friends? or shall we pray that the heavenly powers may aid us to roll away the stones of unbelief that imprison our own spiritual perceptions; and, turning from the material memorials of our friends, seek to feel their presence in the fair places of earth, where we take pleasure, — in the homes, where we enjoyed their companionship?

Sensual grief may be of use to a sensual mind. Mourning garments, funereal pomp, elaborate monuments, may give comfort and a certain kind of consolation to such minds; may, perhaps, induce a seriousness of thought that would not otherwise be attained: but it can hardly be possible that genuine Christian faith could seek or find any thing to satisfy its demands, in the hour of bereavement, in external emblems of grief, that bind the soul to earth, and hinder its upward aspirations.

Among the tombs that have been uncovered in the long-hidden city of Pompeii, there is one which has carved upon it a vessel just anchored, and the seamen furling the sails. It would be difficult to find a truer image whereby to represent the Christian idea of what we call death. Eternity is often compared to the ocean; and the ending of our little life here, to a stream lost in ocean's immensity. There is a forlorn wretchedness in such a comparison, that should give it the lie at once in a Christian mind. The soul's individuality is lost in it; and we feel ourselves homeless as the mind wanders over the unmeasured vastness.

I remember once driving along the sea-shore in the neighborhood of a maritime city, when a great ship came sweeping majestically along the waters, and glided peacefully to its anchorage. "There," said my companion, "is a vessel that has been in the Pacific more than three years." I shall never forget the thrill that passed through me as he spoke. Imagination at once pictured the joy of those who were returning from their weary voyage, and the delight of those who had been so long waiting for them at home. I could have shouted a welcome to them, though they were all strangers; and I envied those who had a claim to give them a friend's greeting. Here was a true picture of a Christian soul, its voyage of this world's life over, anchoring in the heavenly home. Home to the homeless, rest to the weary, peace to the sorrowful, are all implied in the word "death;" and yet we shroud it with gloom, and typify it with the revolting representations of fleshless bones. True, there are wrecks on life's ocean, voyages that terminate in despair; but, as a general rule, it is the termination of the happiest voyage of life that we look upon most tearfully, while we are easily reconciled to the close of one that is worthless. There is, apparently, as little just appreciation of the relations and the value of life and death, in the minds of most persons, as there would be of voyages in one who should weep at seeing a noble ship come home in safety, and smile when a wreck was dashed upon the shore.

It seems to me that the feelings of joy and welcome which naturally arise in the human soul at the sight of a long-absent ship coming safely into port must typify the emotions of the inhabitants of heaven, when they look upon the spirits who are newly arrived from earth. To us who are left behind, there must naturally be sadness for our loss, when those we love pass before us to their eternal home: but a Christian faith must teach us that such feelings are purely selfish; and that, in cherishing them, we are sinning against Him who brought life and immortality to light.

The Jew, who has no assurance of an existence beyond the grave; the Pagan, who is ignorant of the paternal love of the divine Creator,—may well grieve as one who has no hope, when he sees the eyes of his loved ones closed in their last sleep: but, if the Christian refuses to be comforted, his Christianity must be an external faith, and not an internal affection. If we believe that the heavenly Father does not suffer a sparrow to fall to the ground contrary to his will, we cannot believe that a human life is less tenderly cared for. We cannot, then, feel that death is more premature when it comes to the infant of days than to the old man of many years, or that it is less under the divine control in the strife of battle than in the peace of home.

The early Christians recognized the new aspect which the knowledge of immortality gave to the death of the body; and they soon ceased to use the signs of mourning for the dead, that, till then, had been universal. They felt that it was wrong to mourn for the dead; and their epitaphs in the Roman catacombs still testify to the peaceful trust and the hopeful assurance that animated the minds of those who there deposited the mortal remains, often sealed with the blood of martyrdom, of those they held most dear. Among the thousands of inscriptions still to be read there, there is no allusion to be found to the grief of those who were left to perform the last offices for their friends. No inconsolable relatives immortalize their tears on those walls. The simplicity of a childlike faith, that to die here was to live in the mansions of the all-loving Father, seems to have been the abounding source whence flowed the countless phrases that speak of death always as good rather than evil. The bad Latin in which many of the inscriptions are couched proves that a large proportion of the dead were of the lower and little educated classes; but all ranks seem to have been animated by the same spirit. Selfish grief finds no expression there; and the historians tell us, that all signs of mourning in dress were deemed unfitting in those who believed in the Christian immortality.

How long this childlike faith in the new revelation lasted, we do not know: but Protestantism, with its frightful doctrines of election, predestination, and the vindictive wrath of God, was certainly sufficient to crush out all that might have been left of it in the more cheerful faith of Rome; and modern fashion, with its lugubrious ensigns of crape and bombazine, steadfastly testifies how much the sensuous still predominates in the views of death held by society at the present day.

The scientific niceness of the laws which control the time and the manner of mourning, from its first midnight blackness through its gradual shading-off into slate and gray, has so ludicrous a side, that the pen of the satirist and the pencil of the caricaturist find abundant scope for their talent in delineating the shifts and subterfuges of which hypocrisy makes use to simulate a grief it does not feel. True affection, like true piety, may ask, "Why should my neighbor's hypocrisy influence me to refrain from doing honestly what he does dishonestly?" But, if this be really a sign of grief, what has fashion to do with it? If we are just as earnest that our mourning-hat shall be becoming, and in the newest mode, as if it were a ball-room costume, does it not show that the mourning is but a secondary matter? that it is custom and fashion to which we yield, and not grief, when we put on our sable robes? There are fashions which have no moral relations, which are merely harmless conventionalisms; but there are others which involve principles, and which, if those principles be wrong, we cannot follow, and be faithful to our duty. The wearing of mourning for the dead, if mourning for the dead be wrong, is a striking example of such a fashion. Until within a few years, this was a universal custom: but of late, in many of the rural districts, it has gone much out of favor; and close mourning is now a fashion of the town rather than a custom of the land. Still, most persons make some change in their costume when a death occurs in the family circle; and many of those who refrain from the external sign of mourning do so because they look upon it as an extravagant fashion, which should be discouraged by those who can afford it, so that those who cannot may feel that they can abstain from it without being thought wanting in respect for the memory of their friends. This is a good motive; but it is far from being the best motive.

The wearing of mourning is one of the fashions that have a decidedly moral bearing, and is therefore one that should not be followed merely because it is the fashion, and because persons in our particular set will be offended if we fail to adopt it. Nor should we refrain from wearing it merely because we think our example may influence others. Merely external reasons should not control us, because this is not a merely external fashion. It has a moral cause and a moral influence; and therefore the adopting it or the not adopting it should be decided in accordance with the principles of a true morality.

The custom of wearing mourning is one that we share in common with all races and all ages; and it results from the common horror mankind entertain for death. It is essentially an unchristian custom; for one of the grand distinctions of Christianity is, that it presents an entirely new view of death.

The Heathen and the Jew, with whom the life after death is a fearful uncertainty, and death itself a terrible leap into darkness, must mourn with a bitterness that can have little to soften it, when the insatiable grave snatches from them those whom they love; when their friends depart they know not whither, perchance to lie in the cold earth until the last trump shall sound; perchance to lose all personality in a resurrection that shall re-absorb them into the Power that created them; perchance to wander for ever in regions so unlike any thing we can enjoy here, that it is beyond the power of human capacity really to believe in enjoyment there. All this ignorance and uncertainty make it quite excusable in the Heathen and the Jew to mourn, and to carry the signs of mourning to almost any extent; to tear the hair, to cut the flesh, to cover the head with ashes. The advance of civilization has caused these barbaric signs of grief to give place to something less repulsive, although the grief itself seems little changed in character. To disfigure the person is no longer deemed necessary in order to show our respect for the memory of the dead. Provided the hue and the material be right, the milliner and the dressmaker may shape the sombre emblems of woe as becomingly as possible; and personal vanity may find as satisfactory food in crape and bombazine as in the gayer colors and lighter fabrics. Hence no class of the community mourns so deeply in dress as the one that prides itself upon being of the highest elegance, and which holds nice taste in costume to be a cardinal virtue.

A country lady, on entering a fashionable city church, is more struck by the number of ladies in close mourning than by any other difference she sees from what she is accustomed to at home. She says, perhaps, to herself, "We are wiser in this respect, in the country, than the dwellers in the town." Still, the difference is one of fashion, and not of principle. The city ladies wear black, as they wear every thing else, more in extreme than country ladies. So long as the heathenism of mourning is not recognized, they who put on only a little stand on the same plane as those who put on much. The difference is one of degree, and not of kind.

The moral cause for wearing mourning is the want of a distinct and enlightened faith in the life after death. That the dead rise was clearly taught by the Lord, and is believed, or said to be believed, by every one who accepts him as a divine teacher; but after what manner they rise was left to be reasoned out by Christians, in accordance with the light each one possessed. Consequently, theories of a future life are as various as the minds that form them; and the whole subject is looked upon as a matter of theory, and not of faith.

About a century ago, a book was published by Swedenborg, called "Heaven and Hell," in which, for the first time, that which seems to many minds a perfectly logical theory of the future life was taught, and one, at the same time, harmonizing entirely with all that the Scriptures teach us of the character and providence of God. This book has been a great source of comfort to many persons who have never accepted Swedenborg as an authorized teacher, and who receive the doctrines it contains, only in the same way that they would receive the writings of any wise man whose thoughts recommended themselves to their spiritual needs. To those who accepted the peculiar claims of Swedenborg, the truths he taught in relation to the future life came with a power that compelled them to acknowledge that grief for the so-called dead was a selfish passion, which it was the duty of a Christian to resist and put away. This being acknowledged, it followed, that, if the grief were wrong, it was wrong to wear the outward symbols of grief, because they helped to nourish the grief itself, and to make the recovery from it more difficult. They generally, therefore, abandoned the custom. To persons not of their faith, this may seem a merely negative peculiarity; but there is something more, something deeper, in their refusal to follow the fashion of the world in this particular.

Believing, as they do, that the infinite love of the heavenly Father never allows a human being to pass away from the natural world until the best possible time for his entering the spiritual world has come, death never appears to them a premature event; and possessing a faith in the spiritual realities of the other life, built upon what they consider a knowledge of the principles by which that life is arranged and governed, death cannot be to them that indefinable object of terror which it is to those who see nothing but doubt and darkness beyond the grave. Divested of any faith in that far-off judgment-day, when the whole human race, roused by the last trump, shall gather up the poor disintegrated particles of their material frames, and present themselves before a judgment throne to receive their eternal sentence; when all shall long for heaven, but vast multitudes be sent away to an eternity of torment, — divested of this faith, they look forward to an existence beyond the grave, commencing when the soul ceases to animate the body; where no one goes into the life of hell but they who have no love for the life of heaven; where each one seeks out in freedom a mansion adapted to the affections of his individual life; in which, if he be evil, he will be controlled, so that his evil may not impinge upon the freedom of his fellows; and, if he be good, he will go on, through an eternity of joyful progress, in a life that shall perpetually assimilate him more and more to the divine perfection. With a clear and fixed faith in such doctrines, the dying pass away without excitement and without fear; while those who are left behind feel that the time when their friends are putting on the garments of salvation is not the time for them to put on the weeds of woe.

To feel no sorrow that our friends have left us is not to be expected of imperfect humanity. We cannot keep our minds so filled with thoughts of the brighter fate of those who have gone before us, that our hearts will not be sorrowful, or our eyes unmoistened, at the memory of our own loss; but can it be right, can it be any thing but selfishness, if we abandon ourselves to grief, if we nourish it by surrounding ourselves with every external sign of woe? Are we not putting ourselves in opposition to Providence? and have we any right to look to Heaven for strength to bear our bereavements, if we meet them with a belief that it is a virtue in us to cultivate the sense that they are bereavements?

The sting of death is sin. If our friends have lived and died in sin, we may well mourn for them while they live and when they die; but such mourning would naturally conceal itself within the most secret recesses of the heart. If, on the contrary, we have a blessed assurance that our friends have lived and died in the service of the Lord, let us lift up our hearts in thanksgivings that they have gone where the soul's life cannot change its direction, but will go on for ever in the life of grace. Let us be drawn heavenward more and more as the band of friends grows more numerous that awaits us beyond the silent portal; and let us believe, with a lively faith, that that portal opens, not into death, but into life that knows neither disease nor decay nor end. Let us muse upon the blessedness of that life until a holy flame of love shall burn within our hearts, until heavenly light shall illumine our inward eye; and then let us forbear from disfiguring our countenances with sorrow, as though grief were a meritorious passion; and let us not shroud our persons in a raiment appropriate only as an expression of grief that knows no consolation.

The extreme to which the ornamentation of burial-places is often carried is another fashion that has a tendency to interfere with a true view of death. If the dead are risen, why should we linger with impassioned fondness about the spot where the soul's cast-off garment lies mouldering? It may be said that this is but a harmless sentimentalism; but it involves much more than that.

It is hardly possible that one who has a clear, undoubting faith in the spiritual existence of a departed friend, can cling with fondness to the worn-out clothing of that friend's mortality. Such an indulgence of the natural feelings must tend to materialize the mind, and to prevent a living faith in the present, conscious existence of those we mourn. It must prolong the state of mourning in the mind, and impede our growth into that state of acquiescence to the Divine Will which alone can give us true peace in the contemplation of our bereavement. They have forgotten their material bodies : why should we love to remember them? They cannot come down to us in our materialism; but we may lift ourselves toward them by elevating our minds into a true spiritualism.

Departed souls are affected by the state of mind of those whom they have left behind them, though they are as unable to perceive our material bodies as we are to perceive their spiritual ones. The spiritual sympathy between those who have left this world and those who remain in it, must be interrupted and hindered, if one party be absorbed or deeply affected by something that is out of the sphere of the other. Our friends, we certainly hope, are risen into a happy home, freed from disease and material disturbances of every sort, and beginning a course of spiritual growth higher and purer than any thing that could have been attained in this world. They have graduated, as it were, from this lower, preparatory school, because the time had come when it was best for them to go up higher. They still love us, and sympathize with us, and long to help us to come up where they are. Can this love and this sympathy be answered to by us, if, while they are being initiated into those higher pursuits and joys, we are absorbed in the choosing and shaping of garments by which to show how sorry we are that our friends are so lifted up; or if we are haunting, with tearful eyes, the spot where their poor earthly remains lie buried? Is it rational to suppose that they can come to us, and console us with their love, if we indulge in moods of mind so far removed from theirs? Or, if they try to do so, can it fail to mar their happiness in their blessed home? If they strive to linger near us, must it not hold them back in their upward course, if we persist in looking downward? Christian love should make us strive to keep near to our friends by our spiritual elevation, that we may grow with them, and help them to grow, by sympathizing with them, so far as we can, in the new state upon which they have entered. It must needs be that they still turn toward us with affection; and mutual sympathy in heavenly aspirations must mutually strengthen and uphold those aspirations. If we insist upon clinging to all of our friends that belonged to earth; if we dwell with morbid wilfulness upon all that we have lost, and delight in testifying to our grief by all the material signs that dress and sculpture can supply, visiting the tomb as if our friend really rested there, — we can hardly fail to materialize our views of death and of the life after death. By the homage we offer to the dead body of our friend, we may diminish our spiritual consciousness of that friend's now living existence.

"They are not here, they are risen," is the appropriate motto for our burial-places; and those inspired words should be so written on our memories, that they may lift our hearts upward whenever we find ourselves clinging mournfully to material memorials or emblems, that can only chain our thoughts to earth.

Angels rolled away the stone that only seemed to imprison the body of the Lord: let us not pile monuments above the bodies of our friends, as if we would indeed hold them in bonds.

The barren spots, fertile only in thorns and briers, that have been given over to the dead in many places, lack decency, and are unseemly; but, to a Christian eye, a burial-place given over to ostentatious display can hardly be more attractive. Heathenism seems to "reign in triumph here."

Modern times have yet to learn what a truly Christian burial-place should be. Not a place so poor, that it should seem as if the avarice of the living grudged room for the decent disposal of the bodies of the dead; nor yet so fine as to offer a hideous contrast to the decay it covers.

Pride and ostentation meet us everywhere while we live in this world: but let us at least hope that the day may come, even on earth, when a purified Christian taste may learn to perceive that simplicity should reign in the burial-place, if nowhere else; that humility, though little admired elsewhere, is at least becoming at the grave.

MEMORY IN THE FUTURE LIFE.

"Those things which absolutely enter into the life, and become spontaneous, and, as it were, natural, vanish out of the external memory, but remain inscribed on the internal memory, whence they are never blotted out.

"Heavenly and spiritual love give an orderly arrangement to all things belonging to the exterior memory; whereas self-love and the love of the world prevent order, and confuse all things.

"The interior mind of man looks into the things of the natural memory; and those things there which confirm divine truths, it sublimates, as it were, by the fire of heavenly love, and withdraws them and purifies them, till they become spiritual ideas." — SWEDENBORG.

MEMORY IN THE FUTURE LIFE.

WHAT shall we remember of this life, when we enter upon that which is to come? is a question that often forces itself upon the mind; sometimes asked by our hopes, when we dread to lose out of the memory that which we love to dwell upon; and sometimes by our fears, when we tremble lest we may never forget things that we can remember only with pain or remorse.

Memory is a vast storehouse, filled with the most varied possessions. To some persons it is a fair mansion, inhabited by beautiful forms, and vocal with sweet melodies. To others it is a charnel, haunted by grim spectres and discordant sounds. Yet there is probably no one who has not something there he would gladly forget, and much that he would wish always to remember. To forget the past entirely, would seem little less than losing one's identity; yet most, if not all of us, would shrink from remembering it entirely.

The annals of medical and moral science go far towards proving, that what is once written upon the pages of memory is never erased; for the delirium of fever, or the excitement of violent emotion, is known to awaken in the mind the memory of things that no voluntary effort could have recalled, in a state of health or tranquillity.

Many instances are on record, of persons, who, under the excitement of the fear of sudden death by drowning or other violent cause, relate, that, in a few seconds of time, the memory of their whole past lives, even in minute detail, passed through their minds so rapidly as to make seconds seem hours. There is a story related by Coleridge, and believed to be well authenticated, of a woman who could not read, but who, in the delirium of fever, repeated correctly long passages from Hebrew, Greek, and Latin authors, which she had heard read years before by a scholar, as he walked to and fro in a passage-way of his house, having a door opening into the kitchen where she was a servant. A still more striking proof of the permanence of all impressions made upon the memory has been recorded by the principal of one of the schools for the training of idiots. A little girl, seven years old, was brought to him in a state so idiotic, that she had never spoken. Under his tuition, she learned to talk; and, after remaining with him three years, she returned home to visit her family; when, to their surprise, she recognized, and called by name, not only all the members of her own family, but all the neighbors who had been in the habit of coming to the house, but of whom she had never been supposed to take any notice.

Such facts as these make it difficult for us to doubt that all impressions made upon the memory are absolutely indelible. If the dulness of idiocy and the indifference of ignorance are so impressible, we can hardly refuse to believe that the memory of every human being retains, so long as life lasts in this world, every thing that has once been written there.

What effect death may have upon the memory is still an unanswered question in the minds of most persons; and, to those who possess a genuine faith in another life, it must be a question of deep interest. The intellect asks it, as it contemplates the stores of knowledge it has garnered, and would gladly carry away into a wider sphere and increase for ever. The affections ask it, longing to believe that the friendships and the loves that have enriched life here may be renewed and perfected in the life to come. Remorse asks it, longing to forget; and grief asks it, fearing it may remember.

The unsatisfying reply usually given to such questions is, that we must trust in the mercy of the Lord, that all will be ordered for our best good and highest happiness; and that it is unwise in us to trouble our minds with questions that cannot be answered.

It would be difficult to find any question of mental or moral philosophy which has not an answer in the writings of Swedenborg; and memory is an object of especial consideration in them, in its relations both with this life and with the life to come. He tells us that memory is twofold, — external and internal. To the external memory belong all the facts of the material life, considered merely as facts, — its events, its daily cares and employments, its science, its art, and its literature. To the internal memory belong the results of all those facts which have impressed themselves upon the mind so as to become part and parcel of the spiritual being. The internal memory is the "book of life," on the pages of which are written the results of all that we love and think and do while we live in the natural world. The external facts of this life, considered merely as facts, have no permanent interest or value. Their worth lies wholly in the effects they have produced upon the character. These effects build up our spiritual body as food and drink build up the natural body, and form it into the image and likeness of the master whom we choose to serve.

The function of memory in the mind corresponds to that of the stomach in the body. The stomach is a place of deposit for the material food, and there it is digested; and then what is appropriate to the system is assimilated to its various tissues and organs, and what is inappropriate is rejected and thrown aside. In proportion as the food is wholesome, taken in proper quantities, and well digested, the body is filled with life and health and strength. If, on the contrary, the food be unwholesome or imperfectly digested, the body is filled with disease. If too much be taken, the system is clogged and encumbered in its functions; if too little, the strength is wasted, and the body pines away.

The memory performs for the spiritual body a use precisely corresponding to that which the stomach performs for the natural body. It furnishes a storehouse for all the mental food; and the use which this food subserves depends on the power of digestion and of assimilation possessed by the spiritual body.

Closely connected with the function of digestion is that of appetite; and this depends on the health and the habits of the body. It may be deficient or unnatural from weakness or disease; or too great, and craving unwholesome substances, from a habit of over-eating, and disregard to the laws of health. A body that is healthy, and that has been habituated to act upon the principle, that food and drink are the daily bread for which we pray, and which is provided by the Lord to strengthen it for the performance of its daily duties, will desire only such food as is wholesome, and will be content when enough has been taken to satisfy hunger. A body that is unhealthy, or that has been suffered to acquire habits of gluttony and intemperance, is subject to desire unwholesome food, and to eat and drink for sensual gratification, without caring for the use which food was designed to subserve. All these states of the natural body have their corresponding ones in the spiritual body; and the one is built up by assimilating spiritual food, just as the other by assimilating natural food. A mental appetite, hungering for the bread which cometh down from heaven, is the sure index of a spiritual body, healthy in all its functions and habits.

By the bread which cometh down from heaven is not meant direct religious instruction only. Every branch of knowledge that we leaven with the divine truth becomes heavenly bread to us; while the word of God, as it is given to us directly in the Sacred Scriptures, is not heavenly bread for us, if we read it unworthily.

When we study the sciences that illustrate the world around us, believing that this world was fashioned by the hand of God for our instruction, illustrating by correspondences the truths that belong to the spiritual world, the sciences become heavenly bread to us. When we study history, believing that the Divine Providence is over all its events, and that the fate of nations illustrates for us the development of the human soul, both collectively and individually, we make heavenly bread of history. When we study mental philosophy, seeking to understand the workings of the human mind in order better to subdue our own passions, and so bring our whole being into subjection to the laws of the divine Creator, philosophy is heavenly bread for our souls. When we study the Sacred Scriptures that we may learn the commandments of our heavenly Father in order to do and teach them, the Scriptures become the veritable bread of life to us.

Every one of these branches of instruction is capable of being desecrated by our pride and worldliness, so that it may become deadly poison to the spiritual body, and the Bible more than all others; because that which is in itself most holy, becomes, when desecrated, the most harmful. When the love of self and of the world rules in the mind, instruction is sought only that it may minister to our pride and self-complacency. Then the memory becomes a fountain of disease, pouring its poison into all the members of the spiritual body; and, the more it is filled, the lower must the soul sink in the scale of spiritual being.

The facts and truths we learn in our intellectual studies, so far as they are merely such, belong to the external memory, and are forgotten when we put off the material body; but the results we gain from them, when we study them with a view to their relations with the spiritual world and with our own souls, belong to the internal memory, and abide with us for ever.

In like manner, the events of the daily life, that belong only to the external nature, live only in the external memory. What we eat and drink, and wherewithal we are clothed, to-day, have their own importance while this day lasts; but to-morrow we shall have no need to recall them to memory. So far as they were adapted to our healthful nourishment and protection, our food and clothing of yesterday make our bodies vigorous in their functions to-day. The more perfectly they were thus adapted, the less we think about them afterwards; for the healthy body forgets itself. It is only when the functions are imperfectly performed that we are reminded of our bodies. Then the time has come when we should recollect what we have done wrong, in order to avoid the same mistake in future; or what natural wrong tendency there is in our constitution, that we may take measures to reform it.

So in our spiritual bodies: just in proportion as we do our work faithfully every day, we shall forget the past, and refrain from the endeavor to anticipate the future. We never have so little self-consciousness as when we are doing our duty most faithfully. Socrates seems to have recognized this truth: for he says his attendant genius never said any thing to him so long as he did that which was right; but, so soon as he began to do any thing wrong, she reminded him of his delinquency.

Our spiritual body of to-day is formed out of the affections and thoughts and actions of our past life; but we remember each of these very imperfectly. Our spiritual body is healthful in proportion as we have been faithful to the law of the Lord; and, the more healthful it is, the less we think about it. When we have done wrong, remorse torments us with the memory of our sin; but the innocent actions of our lives pass out from the external memory, to be built into the organs and tissues of the spiritual body, filling us with heavenly happiness, which is the consequence of a heavenly life.

When the material body dies, the external memory becomes gradually quiescent; and the internal memory, which is the "book of life," becomes more vividly active than it ever was during its existence in this world. The memory of merely external events and actions falls asleep; while the memory of all things that have become wrought into our spiritual being stands out distinctly in the mind, not to be gainsaid or forgotten.

If we look upon the internal memory as the book of our lives, the pages of which are to stand through eternity, inscribed with what we have written there, it becomes a question of the deepest interest what we shall write upon those pages, and how we shall write it.

The memory takes in every thing that is presented to it through the senses, bad and good. In the daily commerce of life, it has little freedom of choice as to what it shall receive; but it has a choice as to what it will digest, and assimilate to itself. We hear things and see things that fill us with disgust and loathing, and make us feel as if our spiritual body had been poisoned by an impure contagion: but we mistake in this; for it is only the external memory that has been touched. The spiritual body is harmed only by the evil that we love; for it is only love that digests and assimilates what lies in the memory, and so makes it a constituent part of our being. What we remember with aversion cannot be written in the book of our life.

In so much of the daily intercourse of society as is beyond our control, we are not responsible for what our memories receive; but in that intercourse which is of our own seeking, and in the books we read, it is quite otherwise. In these, we are voluntarily giving food to the memory. In these, we select what we love; and this will be transferred to the internal memory, and so become part of the spiritual body which is to live for ever. If what we thus select is impure, the contagion is a defilement to the soul; and the soiled pages of our book of life will bear the testimony of our degradation.

With a still firmer hand, we are making our entries on these enduring pages in all that we say and do. The external life is the embodiment of all that we love; and, so long as we love them, the journal of our words and actions will stand uneffaced. Every thing that we truly repent of is suppressed in the memory when we die; but all that we love is distinctly written there for ever. It is not enough, that, when we suppose death is approaching, we start back in terror from the recollection of our past lives, because we fear the consequences they may bring upon us in the life to come. Fear is not repentance; and remorse that springs only from fear has no power to efface the memory of our sins. They will cling to us until we learn to hate them, because we love the Lord; and then they will pass away, never more to return, unless the love of evil that produced them comes back into the heart. Grief for sin that has been truly repented of belongs exclusively to the external memory. It will remain with us as a warning, to keep us on our guard while we remain in this world: for, when we have once fallen into the commission of any sin, we are liable to fall again; because wrong-doing impairs the strength of the soul, and it is never safe for us to forget the weakness of a member that has once sinned.

In the material body, a wound or broken bone, a sprained muscle, or congestion of a vital organ, leaves the affected part permanently weakened; and fatigue, debility, or exposure to severities of heat or cold, brings back painful symptoms, reminding us that the integrity of the body is impaired.

We do not enter the future life perfect beings, even the best of those who dwell on earth; but that life is one of eternal progress in the direction in which we have walked while here. Therefore there must still be struggle with self, and sorrow for the evil we feel within our hearts, in the other world, similar to that which we feel in this. But those who have truly begun the regenerate life never fall into the commission of sinful actions after they enter the eternal world. So far as they are not perfectly established in the regenerate life, they may be tempted to commit the same evils in the other world that they were liable to in this: but they never fall there; because, the moment that an evil desire rises in the heart, it is provided of the Lord that the external memory should awaken, and the sins of the past life start up, spectre-like, before the mind's eye; and in humility, and anguish of remorse, the soul turns for protection against itself to the Father, who is an ever-present help to those who seek him.

Shall we recognize the friends who have gone before us into the spiritual world? Most certainly we shall. The affections that form the enjoyment of our present life will continue with us when we enter the other, just as vividly as ever. There is no loss of identity, nor of any of the thoughts and affections that go to make up identity, in passing through the portal that separates the material from the spiritual world. The first impulse of the spirit, when it becomes aware that it has passed out from the material body, is usually to seek for the relatives and friends who had preceded it. At first, there is a pleasure experienced in these renewals of friendship, similar to what was felt on earth; but the permanency of attachments in the future life depends upon the absolute characteristics of the soul, far more than it does in this world. Here we understand each other very imperfectly, and are liable to form incorrect estimates of each other. Here we are often deceived by external appearances, and so may form friendships on mistaken judgments of those with whom we associate. In the future life, we know each other much more perfectly, and can never be deceived so far as to mistake good for evil, or evil for good, if we really love goodness ourselves, and desire, in our search after it, to be led by the Lord. Friendship in the future life is based on similarity of moral purpose. A good spirit, therefore, cannot love an evil one; neither can an evil spirit love a good one. Many friendships are formed in this life between the good and the evil: but, though they are renewed in the other life, they are not continued; for the two parties to such a friendship, when they perceive each other as they actually are, stripped of all the external veils of worldly conventionalities, soon feel a mutual repulsion, and no longer desire to continue friends. This is not only so in friendship, but in the love of all the family relations. Every tie of misplaced affection is gradually and gently but surely broken, whether it be of friendship, kindred, or love. There is no force of superior power exerted in these separations; but they are effected by the natural repulsion that must exist between good and evil when each is distinctly manifest.

When a good person knowingly and wilfully forms a friendship in this life with an evil person, as is sometimes the case, it is much more difficult and painful for a separation to take place between the parties, and the progress of the good spirit is much retarded; for, in such a case, there is an evil internal to the friendship which is very difficult to overcome: but, where the good form friendships with the evil through mistaken judgment, the separation is comparatively easy and painless.

The natural mind may shrink from the idea, that brother and sister, parent and child, can forget the tie of blood, and cease from loving each other; but, in the great household of heaven, we may perceive that a relationship must exist higher than that of blood, though parallel with it. What blood is to the natural body, affection is to the spiritual body; and, in the spiritual life, all relationship must depend on similarity of affection. If this does not exist within the love that we feel for our kindred on earth, that love will gradually die out in the spiritual world, and be replaced by something higher and more true. In heaven, all personal affection must be founded on love to the heavenly Father. In heaven, there is but one parent; and all who enter there are the children of one family. We need not forget there the ties of blood that bound us to each other here; but we shall value them less selfishly, less narrowly, in the great fraternity of heaven.

The most absorbing affection of which the human heart is capable, which we are told must supersede all other earthly ties, and which is used in Scripture to typify the connection between the Lord and the Church, is subject to the same laws that govern the relations of friendship and family. If it be founded on the merely external and temporal uses and conventionalities of society, it ceases with the life of this world. To those who look upon it only as a means of selfish and worldly enjoyment or aggrandizement, the Lord says now, as to the Sadducees of old, "In the resurrection they neither marry nor are given in marriage." The angels of heaven can know no *such* connection. The marriage union of eternity is perfect and harmonious as that which exists between the heart and the lungs, between the right eye or hand and the left. Each party seeks the good of the other, finding therein its own most perfect happiness; and both look ever towards the Lord, as the source of every capacity for goodness, and its consequent blessedness and peace. This union is personal as one's own identity, eternal as the existence of the soul.

SPIRITUALISM.

"Woe unto the foolish prophets that follow their own spirit, and have seen nothing!

"They have seen vanity and lying divination, saying, The Lord saith; and the Lord hath not sent them." — Ezekiel.

SPIRITUALISM.

So many bereaved hearts find consolation in the communications obtained through the various signs and sounds of mediums, that it seems to be a legitimate subject of religious inquiry, how far such communications are worthy of credit, and what place they should take among the sources of consolation and instruction vouchsafed to us by Providence.

Scientific men may tell us scornfully, that there are no facts, and religious men may tell us indignantly that there is no truth, in the Spiritualism of the present day; but, still, men and women will throng in crowds to the mediums, and will believe that what they see is fact, and that what they hear is truth.

The universality of a faith in a spiritual Creator of the material world, and of a spiritual existence for man after the material life ceases, has always been regarded as a strong presumptive evidence that such things really are. Still, materially-minded men have been found in all ages, who were ready to deny both these articles of faith.

That spirits who have left the body have power to communicate with spirits still inhabiting the body, is a belief, that, until very recently, was quite as universal as the other two; and is now denied only in communities that have become enlightened by scientific truth. Educated persons are inclined to shrink from any acknowledgment of the possibility, that spirit may in any way make itself manifest to the senses of men and women living in this world, as if it were something shameful, and implying gross ignorance and superstition.

Much of this incredulity is assumed through dread of ridicule; and many believe in their hearts, while they deny with their lips. Too many instances of preternatural communications are authentically recorded in history and biography, too many are handed down orally in families living around us, to allow of any thing like universal disbelief. The most determined deniers are men of science; but it may be reasonably doubted, whether devoting one's mental powers exclusively to the study of the material creation is the best way of illuminating it in spiritual things. All can see the folly of the pope, who had studied only spiritual things, when he undertook to decide that the assertion of Galileo was false; but Galileo would have been as foolish as the pope, if he had assumed that he could measure the powers and capacities of spirits, because he could prove that the earth moved round the sun.

It is easy for us to see that it must have been a superstitious age, when many innocent victims were hurried out of the world by violent and cruel means, because the clergy were allowed to decide upon evidence in matters of life and death, which by no means came within their vocation; but future generations may see as easily, that it must have been a sceptical age, when men of science were deemed the best judges of spiritual things, and an age devoted to materialism as no age ever was before.

Modern scientific discovery has advanced so rapidly, and accumulated facts so fast, that the attention of intelligent minds has been called to the material world more strongly than at any previous period of history; and it is not surprising that the material world should for a time occupy an unduly elevated place, and attract an unduly exclusive attention. Still, the spirit will resist the reign of matter; and the uncultivated majority will not submit to have its so-called superstitions torn from its grasp. Not that all cultivated minds are sceptical, and all ignorant ones superstitious; for there are beautiful exceptions to the scepticism of science, and fearful exceptions to the superstition of ignorance: but, taken as a whole, it can hardly be denied, that the average tendency of science is towards scepticism, and the average tendency of ignorance is towards superstition.

The so-called Spiritualism of the present day has grown so rapidly, since its first beginning, a very few years ago, at Rochester, that thinking minds can hardly abstain from giving some heed to it. When a form of religious faith counts its votaries by millions, it may be doubted if a truly religious mind should be excused for ignoring it, or setting it aside as jugglery or superstition, without first examining its claims with considerable care. That we have a religious belief of our own, which satisfies our faith and our affections, may suffice to set our own minds at rest concerning the claims of any new form of faith: but we cannot stand alone in this world; and the relations we bear to society call upon us to take some decided ground in regard to a belief which is either a corrupting superstition, or the opening of a new mode of intercourse with the world of spirits. If it be the latter, we may desire to become acquainted with it for our own sakes; if the former, we should endeavor to comprehend it so far as to be able to aid others who are liable to be led away by it, or who have already given themselves up to its misguiding influence.

Probably there is no religious denomination, taken as a whole, who have given so little heed to Spiritualism as the class of persons who belong to the New-Jerusalem Church, or, as they are more commonly designated by others, Swedenborgians; and yet the members of this church form the only class of Christians who believe that intercourse with spirits is perfectly possible, and in no way discordant with the laws of nature or the powers of man.

The discoveries of modern science have, one after another, brought their tribute of evidence, each in its own form, to prove the truth of the philosophy and the theology revealed to the world through the instrumentality of Swedenborg; and now Spiritualism, with its lofty flights of fancy and its puerile depths of folly, with its elevated morality and its low hypocrisy and falsehood, forms a heterogeneous whole precisely in accordance with what Swedenborg tells us of the inhabitants of the "world of spirits," or middle country between heaven and hell, where the spirits of the departed go on first leaving the world of matter, and before taking their final places in heaven or hell.

Many persons seem to think, that, if any thing is preternatural, it must be supernatural; that, if any thing comes to us from the region of spirits, it must be pure and true, holy and dignified. Because many so-called spirits are found liars, they decide that the whole thing must be false: for, if it came from heaven, it must be all true; and they are sure God would allow nothing to come to us from hell. Others, after a careful examination, finding it impossible to escape from the evidence of preternatural power, decide, that, because much is false and evil, the whole thing must come from hell.

The doctrines taught by Swedenborg place us upon a middle ground, where we can answer the objections on both sides, and give a rational solution of the whole phenomena of Spiritualism.

According to those doctrines, the spiritual world is divided into three regions, — the world of angels, or heaven; the world of spirits; and the world of devils, or hell. All spirits, immediately upon leaving their material bodies, pass into the second of these regions, and there remain until they are made thoroughly to understand themselves, and to decide of their own free will whether they will choose heaven or hell for their final abode; for man is not promoted to heaven nor cast down to hell by the arbitrary judgment of the Almighty. His own thoughts and affections pass judgment upon him, and by them he is led to choose a home with spirits like himself. If his thoughts and affections are heavenly, they lead him naturally to desire and enjoy the society of angels; while, to those whose thoughts and affections are infernal, such society would be a grievous bondage, and they flee away from all that is heavenly, and find themselves at home only in the regions of hell. The duration of the residence of spirits in this middle country is very various. Those who have been very good or very evil in this world go soonest to their final homes; while those whose characters have been less marked, and who do not readily learn to know the dominant inclinations of their own natures, remain sometimes for many years before they are able to acknowledge to themselves the ruling loves which were dominant with them in the flesh, and which must remain dominant when the flesh is cast off: for, in this world, we all make our final choice of the direction in which we shall walk through all eternity; though, with many, the life seems so vacillating and uncertain, that, to finite perceptions, it may appear that there is as great an inclination in one direction as in the other.

The inhabitants of this middle region are the only spirits who can readily hold direct intercourse with persons still living in this world. The spirits who are in heaven or hell are too far removed in the plane of their life from us to be able to make themselves manifest to us, excepting in very rare and peculiar instances. These spirits are as varied in character now as they were before they left this world. They awoke in the other life possessed of just the same affections as when they fell asleep for the last time here; neither wiser nor better for having passed through the gate of physical death. They have been admitted neither to heaven nor hell, and are incompetent to instruct us about either. A little reflection might lead us to suppose that it would be those spirits who are least capable of instructing who would be most ready to take upon themselves the office of instructors. Recently departed from this world, and as yet knowing little of the world into which they have entered, the candid, the humble, and the truly wise, would feel that they were incompetent to instruct those they had left behind them; while the superficial, the conceited, and the talkative would be all ready to hold forth to whomsoever would listen. Pride and conceit, and love of dominion, that led them to delight in influencing others while in the flesh, continue to make them delight in exercising a still stronger influence, now that they are in the spirit, upon those who are still in this world; and who suppose them to be more competent to instruct, merely because they have gone to a world to them unseen. The love of gossip, too, so intense in many who are around us, cannot become annihilated by the change of abode; but must and the keenest enjoyment in bewildering the minds of inquisitive men and women, who receive any news from the other world, however stale and unprofitable, with open-eyed wonder. Swedenborg tells us, that evil spirits especially delight in exercising power over others; that, when they approach a person, they perceive whatever is in his memory, and are thereby able to exert an influence over him of which they would otherwise be incapable. This agrees with one feature that is constantly observed in the spiritual communications of the present time. So surprising a knowledge of things in the mind of the questioner is often shown, that faith is at once enlisted to believe any thing the spirit may assert. By thus, as it were, compelling the faith, and destroying the rational liberty of the mind, the spirits prove themselves evil; for no good spirit wishes to compel faith, but desires, like the Lord, to leave us all in rational liberty. Spirits who strive to destroy the liberty of the mind are Jesuitical and diabolical.

Again: Swedenborg says that evil spirits are very fond of assuming to be some great person, or some person other than they really are, as the case may be, in order that their words may exert a stronger influence on those to whom they speak. Judge Edmonds, with an amusing simplicity, relates that the spirits told him, that, finding men were more ready to ask who they were than what they had to say, they assumed such names as they thought would carry weight with them, in order to make people more ready to receive what they wished to tell them. It does not seem to occur to the mind of Judge Edmonds, that the spirits who assumed to be Swedenborg and Lord Bacon were playing him the same trick; although there was nothing in what they said that could have enabled a reader to tell which was which, had it not been for the signatures; or that would have led him to imagine that any great mind was uttering itself, unless the most long-winded verbosity be a sign of greatness.

The communications that have been published to the world exhibit an amount of wisdom not at all above the average of what we find in persons dwelling about us; and this is precisely what we have a right to expect, if we assume Swedenborg's doctrines to be true. There is no department of literature at the present day more flat, unphilosophical, and unworthy of notice, than that of the published spiritual communications that have been given to the world. The more intelligent votaries of Spiritualism assure us, that we should not judge of the subject by its printed literature; for the most interesting and valuable communications have never been published, but are scattered about the country in manuscripts that the possessors esteem far too sacred to permit them to meet the public eye. It is very probable that the owners of these writings value them thus highly, but exceedingly improbable that they are really so valuable. Manuscripts, especially those in which we have a personal interest, generally seem more precious than published compositions; and, if these papers were all given to the world, it is probable that the average amount of wisdom they contain would vary little from that of which the public has already been permitted to judge.

Many will naturally be led to ask, why the communications received through Swedenborg should be esteemed any more worthy of credit than those of other mediums. The manner in which he was instructed was entirely distinct from any thing that has been done since his day. The instruction received by the spiritualists comes to them from spirits who are pressing into the material world, eager to display the knowledge they possess, and seeking to take possession of men's minds, and compel their faith by astonishing them with the tricks of jugglers and fortune-tellers.

Swedenborg, on the contrary, was elevated by the Lord into the spiritual world. His spiritual perceptions were opened after the manner of St. Paul, and he saw and heard what was passing in the spiritual world.

The mediums are like persons, who, wishing to know about England, should approach its coast, and think to acquire a knowledge of its geography, its institutions, and its customs, by talking with the pilots, fishermen, or land-sharks, who came off to them in boats. Swedenborg is like a man who has spent years in traversing England in every direction; in conversing with its people of every class; in studying its laws and customs, its arts and sciences, its mineral, vegetable, and animal productions.

The spiritualists give us disjointed, fragmentary information of the most contradictory character, much of it puerile, and much in direct opposition to the Scriptures. Swedenborg gives us an elevated, logical, coherent system, harmonizing perfectly with itself, with science, and with revelation.

Swedenborg gives us no doctrine on the authority of any spirit or angel, but received all the doctrines he teaches by direct illumination from the Lord while reading the Holy Scriptures. The relations of things heard and seen in the spiritual world, interspersing most of his works, illustrate the doctrines, but do not in any case originate them.

The undignified modes by which the spirits manifest themselves is often brought forward as a reason for disbelieving that what is done is the work of spirits: but dignity is by no means a common trait in the beings who dwell on earth; and there is no reason for supposing that passing into the world of spirits induces dignity. It would certainly destroy the identity of a vast multitude of human beings who go hence, if this noble trait of character should be at once bestowed upon them. If we take the only rational presumption, — which is, that we rise up in the world of spirits with exactly the same human soul with which we lie down in the world of matter, — we see at once, that the communications, both in manner and matter, are just what we have a right to expect; just as conceited, just as commonplace, just as gossiping, just as puerile, as they naturally would be, coming from spirits slow to learn, but eager to teach; unwilling to listen, but eager to talk. Spirits who are really wise have something better to do than to spend their time in gratifying the idle curiosity of anybody who is ready to give a dollar that he may spend an hour in talking with them. The readiness with which they play into the hands of those who would thrive by their means, and who are ready to add all manner of tricks of their own to those which the spirits can perform to amuse the curious, is sufficient proof of their belonging to a very low order of beings. The most zealous followers of the spirits are compelled to acknowledge a large proportion of them to be egregious liars; but still they are lured on to believe every thing the spirits may utter which they cannot disprove, and which pleases their credulity.

The efforts that have been made to prove that public mediums are impostors have had a surprisingly slight effect upon the public mind. In various cities, the most gross deception has been proved upon persons following this vocation; and doubtless there are some, who, in consequence, turn away in disgust, and abandon the pursuit of information obtained by such means. Still, Spiritualism increases, year by year and month by month, with a rapidity even greater than that of Mormonism.

The whole mode of operation by public mediums seems to be arranged for deception; and it is not probable that any one who exhibits in public can long retain honesty. Intelligent and honest private mediums exhibit a power in the broadest daylight, incomparably more surprising than the feats performed in darkness by the public mediums; and as different in character, also, as daylight is from darkness. The private medium has not the temptation to deceive that the public one must have. The facility with which communications can be obtained depends very much on the state of health of the medium, and on various other causes, some known and some unknown. If the medium exerts his power in private, and without pecuniary reward, he feels at liberty to confess at any time, that he is not in a state to use his power; but if he makes it a matter of emolument, even in private circles, and, still more, if he undertakes to operate before a public audience, he is often tempted to pretend to put himself in communication when the power is wanting, and to blind the eyes of spectators by tricks, and mislead their minds by subterfuges, when he can give them nothing genuine.

In the Scriptures, all appeals to spirits, for any purpose, are constantly classed as a sin with idolatry; and it is always asserted or implied, that, when we turn ourselves towards spirits, we turn ourselves away from God. Thus, in Deut. xviii. 10–12, we read: " There shall not be found among you any one that maketh his son or his daughter to pass through the fire, or that useth divination, or an observer of times, or an enchanter, or a witch, or a charmer, or a consulter of familiar spirits, or a wizard, or a necromancer; for all that do these things are an abomination unto the Lord."

In the enumeration of the sins of Manasseh, 2 Kings xxi. 5, 6, it is stated that he built altars for all the host of heaven, and used enchantments, and dealt with familiar spirits and wizards. Again: in 2 Kings xxiii. 24, we are told in praise of Josiah, that he put away familiar spirits and wizards and images and idols, and all the abominations that were spied in the land. In Isa. xix. 3, we find the same classification of those who " seek to the idols, and to the charmers, and to them that have familiar spirits, and to the wizards." In Leviticus, these same sins are classed together, and forbidden; with the reason appended, " for I am the Lord your God."

These passages all cohere as one, and plainly indicate that the seeking after preternatural knowledge, such as might be obtained from any other sources than those appointed by God, is, in fact, turning away from him. He has given us the Scriptures, and has manifested himself personally for the instruction of his children in doctrine and in life; and, if we seek after knowledge by climbing up some other way, we do it with the assurance that we are committing an abomination in the sight of our God.

It is a singular feature in the religion of the present day, that the authority of the Bible is not considered of the slightest weight in proving the possibility of spiritual intercourse, by a large proportion of persons who assume to be Christian believers. To quote its words in an argument upon the subject, is to provoke a cavil or a sneer or a self-complacent smile, that seems to say, "How can you be so credulous as to consider commands of any authority that I have so entirely outgrown?"

It has been asserted in regard to these texts, that the obtaining access to the spirits must be impossible, or it would not have been forbidden; because there could be no harm in it. The novelty and ingenuity of this reasoning is worthy of all admiration. That a sin should be forbidden us because we cannot commit it, is a mode of legislation so curious, that it could have occurred to none but a subtle reasoner to have ventured upon the suggestion. It may be asked, why this prohibition should be classed apart from all others?—

why, when we certainly are able to commit, and very liable to wish to commit, all other acts prohibited in the Scriptures, this alone is to be torn from its connection, and set by itself as an impossible sin?

A little observation of the effect produced upon the mind by intercourse of this sort would be sufficient to show why it was deemed necessary that it should be forbidden. We are placed upon this earth in order that we may become prepared for heaven; and the spiritualism of Swedenborg teaches us, that to esteem the means of moral progress and culture, which the world affords us, of little worth, is to undervalue the only means by which regeneration can be obtained. The faithful performance of the duties set before us here by our heavenly Father is the only way in which we can fit ourselves for performing the heavenly duties that await us in the world hereafter.

The state of mind produced by seeking after the wisdom of the spirits is adverse to the performance of the common duties of life. The mind is filled with curiosity, and is continually seeking to gratify it by appealing to the spirits; and, the more constant the intercourse becomes, the less willing is the mind to turn itself towards temporal things, and to see in them the stepping-stones to a higher life. It is a received doctrine with the spiritualists, that, to become a good medium, it is necessary to withdraw one's self from intercourse with the world as much as possible, and live in a sort of ascetic retirement, free from material care. Swedenborg tells us, that this mode of life induces a state of nervous excitement, that renders one susceptible to the influences of a fantastic class of spirits, who are sure to mislead all who trust to them.

Some men who take up arms against Spiritualism start from the position, that it is impossible for spirit to manifest itself in any way to mortals. They seize upon certain things done by spiritualists which they can imitate, and cry out, "This is nothing; we can all do it!" but take not the slightest notice of the things done which they cannot imitate. Such *ex-parte* evidence against a criminal would be driven from our courts of justice with opprobrium: but any thing seems to them sufficient to convict a medium of falsehood; and, if one medium is false, they assume that all mediums must be the same. Probably nine-tenths of the feats performed by public mediums are mere tricks for obtaining money, and have nothing to do with any spiritual being; but there is a class of facts developed in private, by mediums who are among the purest minds in the country, which can be explained by none of the theories that have as yet been offered, and which admit of no explanation but a spiritual one.

The question is often asked, how it can be possible that the Almighty would permit evil and dangerous spirits to come back to earth, and use their influence to the detriment of the souls of those who seek them. There seems to be a good deal of confusion in the minds of many persons regarding what God permits and what he approves. Thus they think he would not permit spiritual intercourse, unless he approved it. Yet we all know that he permits the earth to be infested with every form of sin; and we know as well, that he disapproves it far more than we do. He desires to give us entire liberty; and it is this liberty that constitutes us responsible beings. If we are not entirely free to choose between good and evil, we cannot be justly accountable for what we do. The objector would again, perhaps, ask how it can be that he permits this new mode of intercourse between this world and that to come for no useful end. To this the New Church replies, that spiritual intercourse is not a new thing; that it has existed, in some form or other, ever since the world began. While the Scriptures were received as the absolute word of God, the Jewish and the Christian churches both recognized two distinct modes of this intercourse, — one holy and sacred, which came to mortals without their seeking, and which constituted them seers and prophets for the benefit of the Church; the other, impure and selfish, sought out by the individual for his own benefit, or for the gratification of his curiosity, which the Church regarded as a sin, and the State punished as a crime. Rationalism and materialism at length became dominant: every thing spiritual was driven so far off from the minds of men, that, for a while, all voluntary turning towards the objective reality of the world of spirits ceased; although extraordinary dreams and visions have continued to occur often enough to prevent the entire loss of faith in a spiritual world among the great body of the people. At length, the pendulum having swung to the utmost limit the minds of men could bear in one direction, it swings back as far the other way. All legal restraints being removed, men and women rush madly, by thousands, to seek the spirits; and the low and impure spirits, who are near enough to the material world to feel its influence with sufficient power, come willingly to meet them. No new principle is developed by all this, no new power exercised: it is only that humanity has suddenly taken a fancy to make use of a power it always possessed, but never before used with so much freedom. The objector urges, that he cannot believe the great minds that have passed away from earth are ready to come back, and discourse of the unseen world, at the call of the ignorant and the impure. The New Church answers, that when the low, the impure, and the ignorant call, the spirits of former mortals of the same classes come; and, being shrewd enough to know that they would have little or no influence if they confessed their own insignificance, they claim to be the great ones of the earth, and so command the attention of listening crowds.

How far it may be desirable to convert to Spiritualism those who believe the gulf impassable that separates the embodied from the disembodied spirit, is a difficult question. The conviction that a vast mischief was being done by the spirits to the minds of many well-intentioned persons, by upsetting their faith in Scripture and their love for the true and the right, has made it seem desirable to set forth some of the views of the New Church, hoping thereby to lend a helping hand to those who are in danger of falling a prey to the spirits, or who have already fallen, by endeavoring to show that they are as little to be trusted now as in the days of Saul or of Cæsar; that they who attempt to penetrate the world of spirits through human means are leaning upon a staff that may break, and pierce the hand; and that, if we would walk surely and safely, we must "seek not unto them that have familiar spirits, and unto wizards that peep and mutter, but unto the Lord our God."

THE

BUILDING-UP OF REGENERATE LIFE.

789889 A

"Pride is base, from the necessary foolishness of it; because, at its best, when grounded on a just estimation of our own elevation or superiority above certain others, it cannot but imply that our eyes look downward only, and have never been raised above our own measure. For there is not the man so lofty in his standing or capacity, but he must be humble in thinking of the cloud habitation and far sight of the angelic intelligence above him, and in perceiving what infinity there is of things he cannot know, nor even reach unto, as it stands compared with that little body of things he can reach, and of which, nevertheless, he can altogether understand not one; not to speak of that wicked and fond attributing of such excellency as he may have to himself, and thinking of it as his own getting, which is the real essence and criminality of pride." — Ruskin.

THE BUILDING-UP OF REGENERATE LIFE.

CURIOSITY seems to be the first intellectual trait that wakens into life in the mind of a child. The first movements of his intelligence are directed towards discovering the *properties* of the various objects that surround him: the second movement is to ascertain their *causes*. He every day sees the persons around him making various things, and it presently occurs to him that every thing must have been made by somebody. When he is told in regard to the objects of nature, that they were made by God, he next inquires how and why God made them. As a general thing, every succeeding reply that is given is calculated to turn his mind away from God, instead of leading him to recognize the creating and sustaining power of the Almighty by teaching him to feel that the Divine Presence, everywhere at hand, is all that we can know of existence, life, and growth.

The child asks, perhaps, where the trees come from; and is told that they grow out of the ground. Next he asks what makes the trees grow out of the ground. If he receive the simple answer, "God makes them," he is told the sum and substance of all he can ever learn. Here, where the most illiterate begin, the most learned are forced to end. All that we can learn further of the life and growth of a tree is merely a series of facts in relation to the means by which the Almighty works; but no one step has ever been taken towards understanding how life and growth are imparted to the inorganic substances out of which the tree is made. The child is probably told a few facts, such as he can receive, about the sowing of seed; and how the moisture of the earth and the warmth of the sun combine to make the seed germinate, and send roots downward, and leaves upward; and how the roots suck up moisture, which becomes sap in the plant, and feeds it, and makes it grow. If he have a dull mind, he probably rests here all his life; and it never occurs to him that he does not understand all about how plants grow. If his mind be an active one, as he grows older he pushes his investigations a little farther, and, by observation and study, finds out many more facts; but they are still all on the same plane with those that he first learned when a child. They are all facts which are learned through the perceptive faculties, and of which he has no more understanding than the most ignorant clown.

The naturalist continues his observations as far into the secrets of the interior construction of plants as the power of the microscope can carry him, and discovers a minute organization of cells and dots, which he supposes to be the earliest form of organic life, and finds that the plant increases in size by a propagation of these cells one from another: but still it is only a form of life, not life itself, he has found; a consequence of growth, not its power. The naturalist, in all this investigation, has not risen above the plane on which the rustic stands. His plane, it is true, is a little wider; but it is no higher. His facts are all facts of sensuous perception; and his having acquired them through a microscope in no wise elevates their character.

The mother, wearied with the "hows" and the "whys" of her child, distracts his attention by showing a new plaything, or by doing something new with an old one; and the child presently forgets what he has been asking about. So the naturalist, when the student asks him to explain the phenomena of life and growth, shows him beautiful diagrams of cells and dots; and the student, in his admiration of the skill of the professor, forgets what he has been asking, and fails to perceive that consequences are not causes. Not unfrequently, the youthful student, still standing in the outer courts of discovered science, is heard flippantly declaring, that he believes nothing which he does not understand, when some topic of religious faith is under discussion, unconscious that idiocy alone can exist in the state which he assumes for himself; for, the moment we believe any fact in relation to the external world, we believe something that we do not, and that we never can, understand. Men more advanced in learning too often make this same absurd assumption: so that it is common to hear men of science spoken of as a class less religious than any other. Such men claim every novel fact or principle they may discover, with as much conceit as if it were something of their own creation, with which the Almighty had nothing to do.

Noble examples, however, are to be found among the wisest men of science, and those who have done most to widen the fields of knowledge, who clearly perceive the incapacity of the human mind to understand the facts it discovers in the domain of nature; and who, when most elevated, are most ready to return to the faith of the little child, and to believe with the whole heart that God is everywhere. Gravitation, instinct, life, and all the secret powers which narrower minds look upon as dead laws, perhaps created fortuitously, or, if created by God, long since abandoned of him, and now acting of themselves, a more enlarged understanding perceives, can be nothing else save the divine Omnipotence present everywhere, a universal Providence.

The questions which children ask about God, about death, about the life after death, and about their own souls, are those which parents find most difficult to answer; and few children get any satisfactory replies to their inquiries in relation to these topics. As they advance in life, they generally cease to ask them, perhaps cease to think about them, until they even forget that they ever thought of or were curious in regard to them. Parents and teachers commonly believe that this class of subjects is more difficult of comprehension than that which relates to the external world; but the difference between the two is one of knowledge, and not of understanding. We know more facts about the world of sense than about the world of soul; therefore it is easier talking about it: but we understand no more of the one than of the other.

The science of religion is the soul of the science of matter; and to possess the latter without the former is merely to possess a dead corpse. A dead corpse is, in an anatomical point of view, an object of great interest; but it is an object of interest only because it has been once alive, and its various organs were once subservient to the various vital functions. We study the dead body in order that we may know something about the living body; and we should study inanimate nature in order to obtain light in relation to animate nature; and this, again, that we may learn something about intellectual and moral nature.

In all these studies, it should be borne constantly in mind, that all we can do is to know, and that to understand is something to which we do not attain in any department of science. The scoffer sneers at religious doctrines, *he says*, because he cannot understand them; and he supposes he is speaking the truth. He should say that he does not accept religious doctrines, because he cares nothing about them. Truth is received just so far as it is loved, and no farther. Love opens and quickens the perceptions in whatever direction we look. The want of love is the only limitation to the mind's activity.

It is as foolish in the man of natural science to sneer at the man of religious science, as for the theologian to sneer at the naturalist. By his vocation, if he have devoted himself exclusively to his own department, each has unfitted himself to judge of the faith of the other. A true generalization of all science shows the mutual relations and interdependence of the whole, and banishes all inclination to disdain from every mind, by teaching that he who truly learns any science must be taught of God.

There are three kinds of men in the world, — natural men, rational men, and wise men. Truths also are of three kinds, — truths of sensuous perception, truths of deduction, and truths of life. The man who receives only truths of perception is a natural man, the man who receives truths of deduction is a rational man, and the man who receives truths of life is a wise man. Men are natural and rational according to their intellectuality; they are wise or foolish according to their morality: and the mode in which each individual pursues, receives, and applies the kind of truth that he loves, decides whether he be wise or foolish.

There is a homely proverb, that "a fool knows what he knows; but a wise man knows what he does not know." In other words, a wise man knows the limitations of his own knowledge; while the fool shows his folly by striving to appear to know, or really thinking that he knows, that of which he is, in truth, ignorant.

The distinctive difference between wisdom and folly lies in character, and not in ability; in the morality, and not in the intellectuality. No one can imagine a silly angel. Folly cannot inhabit heaven. The foundation and the superstructure of folly is conceit, — the assuming to know something of which one is ignorant. No man acts or talks foolishly so long as he confines his conversation and his activity to subjects with which he is acquainted.

The cobbler in the story was more knowing in his own vocation than the painter; but when, elated by having proved the painter incorrect in his delineation of a shoe, conceit induced him to criticise a point of art which he knew nothing about, his folly became apparent; and the painter, who had just showed his own wisdom by pretending to no knowledge of shoemaking, and submitting to be criticised by one in most respects his inferior, turned upon him with the merited rebuke, which has since passed into a proverb: "Cobbler, stick to thy last."

The painter and the cobbler typify the wise and the foolish all the world over. None are created foolish; and it is only when under the dominion of vanity that we become so. The fool is ever wise in his own conceit. Those who love the truth, and are willing to pass for just what they are, are wise, each in his own vocation. Those who are indifferent to the truth, and who desire to appear what they are not, are foolish, each by aiming to seem wise in that which is not his vocation.

The wise man seeks instruction for its own sake: the foolish man seeks it for the sake of applause. A foolish man is puffed up by what he knows: a wise man is humbled by the consciousness of what he does not know. The foolish man is constantly looking back with self-complacency upon the limited fields of science he has already traversed: the wise man is ever looking forward to the boundless regions of knowledge that lie before him, as yet unattained. The narrowest intellect is wise, so long as it confines itself to topics with which it is really acquainted: the profoundest intellect is foolish, so soon as it attempts to expatiate on things about which it is ignorant.

The tendency of the present age is to elevate the material above the spirtual. Natural science is cultivated almost to the exclusion of moral and theological science. Scientific schools are rising up in all parts of the world, and the number of scientific students increasing every year; while the complaint comes from the halls of philosophy and divinity, that the number of their votaries is every year diminishing. In ancient times, it was esteemed disgraceful in a philosopher if he applied his science to any purpose of practical utility: in modern times, the philosopher who confines his investigations to the world of thought and feeling is looked upon with contempt, as a useless dreamer. Materialism invades the kingdom of the spirit; and the doctrines of theology are rejected, unless they can be proved by mathematical formularies. This seems to be a natural re-action from the superstition and blind subservience to authority which preceded it. Formerly, theological science fulminated anathemas against natural science; and now natural science takes its revenge by ignoring, denying, or ridiculing theological science.

The theologic age and the scientific age are each equally removed from the true stand-point, which here, as in all lesser things, lies in the midst between the two extremes. Society, like the individual, passes through its several stages of growth. There is the childhood of unhesitating faith in the unseen and in the traditions of the elders; then comes the doubting period of youth, when every thing must be touched and handled, and nothing is too sacred to be questioned; and then mature age, when the seen and the unseen are perceived to be equally real, and equally worthy of faith, mutually dependent, and each illustrative and explanatory of the other.

The individual who never goes beyond the age of unquestioning faith always remains a child; while he who rests permanently in a state that believes only what his senses tell him, though he has passed the period of childhood, has not become a man.

There are three planes of development in the human mind, — the scientific, the intelligent or rational, and the wise or affectional. The first is developed by knowledge, the second by reason, and the third by leading a life in harmony with our knowledge and our reason.

Every man who aims at success in life must educate himself on each of these three planes. By his perceptive powers, he must gather a store of knowledge; by his intellectual powers, he must reflect upon what he knows, and draw from it rational principles; and, by acting in harmony with these principles, he must prove himself wise.

The practical man of business must do all this, if he would rationally hope for success. The farmer, the merchant, the mechanic, must all know their business; must decide by their reason what is the best way of pursuing it; and then must act accordingly, or else they must look forward to failure and disgrace. So it is with the learned professions; so it is with scientific pursuits. In all departments of life, we must know, we must reason, and we must act; and it is not till action has set its seal upon what we know and reason about, that the true quality of the character discovers itself, — that it can truly be discerned whether we are wise or foolish.

In order to attain to religious development, we must go through a similar process. God reveals himself to our senses in the material creation, to our reason in the Scriptures, and to our affections in the personal intercourse he holds with each one of us in the daily circumstances and on-goings of our lives. Unless we study him faithfully and lovingly in each of these revelations, we cannot arrive at a comprehensive idea of religious truth and duty, which will enable us to lead lives of Heaven-directed wisdom.

It is a commonly received opinion, that we become religious without special study or thought; by some inward working of the Holy Spirit in connection with the mind, we know not how; and that study impedes rather than helps religious life. The kind of religion thus developed may be seen at camp-meetings and in religious revivals, so called, — fevers and deliriums of the mind, almost always directly opposed to every thing like healthy, religious life. The rationalism and transcendentalism, which, in opposition to this, sap the foundations of religious faith among the intellectual, result from a man-worship, that seeks the truth in itself, or at the lips of some popular idol, instead of looking to the word of God.

It is a strange, popular fallacy, that we are not responsible for the religious doctrines we hold; and that we may adopt views, merely because they are pleasing to us, on subjects of all others the most dignified in themselves, and the most important to our eternal welfare. Any man would be accounted a simpleton, who should adopt theories, in any worldly science, with as little care and thought as most persons use in their choice of a religious faith. The children of this world still continue to be wiser in their generation than the children of light. To know and to understand, before attempting to do, is but a common act of prudence in all undertakings of a worldly nature; and why should we expect to be able to lead a wise, religious life by intuition? We should rather follow up the search after religious life with fear and trembling, that we may not oppose the working of the Lord within us, which enables us to will and to do. The assurance that the Lord works within us in this matter, should not weaken, but stimulate, our own endeavors; for, if we fall dead weights upon his hands, we mar and interupt his work. We need his aid as much in the performance of our daily duties as in the formation of our religious opinions; and we should look to him for light, and lean upon him for support, as entirely in one case as in the other, but ever working earnestly ourselves. It is for the want of this faith in, and reliance upon, the Lord, as an ever-present teacher and helper, that religious opinion is so at loose ends, so scattered abroad, so without form or comeliness; and it is from the same want that we have so much unfaithfulness in the trades and professions and domestic lives of humanity.

An artisan who really believed that the Lord's eye was upon him would hardly dare to do his work unfaithfully. The merchant would hardly dare to write a lie to his correspondent, if he believed the Lord was looking over his shoulder. The lawyer would hardly pledge the powers of his reason and eloquence to the service of falsehood, if he felt that the Lord was listening to every word that passed his lips. The preacher could hardly utter rhetorical flourishes in the form of prayer, for the entertainment of his human audience, if he really believed the divine Ear was hearkening to his words; or dazzle and bewilder their minds with flashing wit, biting sarcasm, and brilliant sophistry, if he felt himself to be a minister of God, bound to preach God's truth, and not his own fancies. In domestic life, too, if it were believed that the heavenly Father stood in the midst of the household, parents could hardly be so careless of their duties, so regardless of the consequences of their actions; children could hardly be so insubordinate as we too often see them. Falsehood, dissension, selfishness, and all the demons that make home other than a type of heaven, must vanish away before an acknowledged divine presence.

So long as a child is held in the faith of the immediate presence of a superhuman, benignant Being, who knows all his thoughts, and is ready to help him in all his troubles, it is comparatively easy to restrain his passions, and to subdue him to obedience. The intercourse of life soon teaches him to ignore this truth, as so many others do; and then begins his downward course. Not until he returns to that implicit faith of his childhood through the absolute conviction of his reason, can he come into the regenerate life. Through such faith only can he be taught of God, and so enabled to fulfil God's law.

Faith in and obedience to the one only living God is the burden of the teachings of the whole Bible. In the Old Testament, these teachings are enforced by hope of reward, and fear of punishment. In the New Testament, in addition to these, we are appealed to in the name of personal love. His love for us being revealed, we are called upon in turn to love Him with the whole strength of heart and soul; and this, we are told, is the first and greatest commandment. In direct opposition to this, there is a constant effort going on in the world so to destroy faith in a personal God, that there is nothing left for us to love; and to keep this first and greatest commandment becomes impracticable. Then it is asserted, that the all of religious life is the keeping of the second commandment, — "Thou shalt love thy neighbor as thyself." Leigh Hunt has embodied this sophistry in his elegant little poem of Abou Ben Adhem; and probably no bit of moral poetry in the English language has been oftener or more approvingly quoted, during the years that have passed since it first appeared: yet it would be difficult to find any thing, pretending to virtue, which offers a more flat contradiction to the express words of Christ. Abou Ben Adhem does not love the Lord; but he loves his fellow-men so well, that the Lord loves him better than anybody else. The rational and philanthropic morality of the present day is simple Abou Ben Adhemism. It ignores God and his providence as much as possible, and tries to satisfy its conscience by loving its neighbor well enough to answer for both. It rushes headlong into all manner of reformatory movements,— educational, moral, charitable, or political; but, in its strivings after the great and the impossible, it is very apt to trample upon the lesser and the possible which stand in its way. It is so sure of its own rectitude, that it does not acknowledge as its neighbors those who differ in opinion from itself. Having no faith in a particular Providence, it looks with comparative indifference upon the duties which surround it at home, and is ever seeking greater opportunities somewhere else. It has not time nor inclination nor faith to study the workings of Providence in its relations with the human race, in order that it may learn how to be perfect after the manner in which the heavenly Father is perfect; but must work out every thing in a way of its own. Self-assertion is written upon all its movements; an egotism that will not be silenced nor concealed.

Worship is so innate a tendency of every human being, that we can never escape from it; and, so fast as we turn from one object, we always turn towards another. No sooner do we cease to worship a personal, divine Being, than we set up an idol. Some human favorite, perhaps, usurps the throned place in the heart, where only Divinity should sit; or, it may be, our own intelligence becomes our god. If unintellectual in our tastes, we sink into some form of sensuous idolatry; making money, position, fashion, dress, luxury, or any other dominant desire we may have, an idol, before which we bow perpetually, consecrating to its service the first-fruits of all our thoughts and affections.

This is no exceptional picture. Every human being has a temple within his heart, in which an object of worship sits enthroned, before whom he offers perpetual gifts of all that he is and all that he has. If the living God be not there, then Mammon, in some one of his Protean forms, has usurped the place. The man of pure intellectuality is apt to imagine himself morally superior to those who labor only for material gain; but, if his aim be only to obtain the honors and emoluments of this world, he is but a slave of Mammon, after all. Or if he study simply for the gratification of his own taste, living apart from the world, he leads a life of pure selfishness.

All worship is divided between three objects, — God, individual man, and the world. The worship of the world, of one's self, or of some other human being, develops only the lower and more external part of our nature. The most internal and highest part of the soul can only be brought to conscious life through communion with the Holy Spirit. It lies closed, inert, and, as it were, dead, until the outer soul, through humble obedience to the divine law, becomes capable of receiving the divine doctrines. Then the Holy Spirit is breathed into it; and, if it resist not the incoming light, it comes forth like one risen from the dead; weak, uncertain, trembling with a new joy which it fears may be but a passing emotion or a transient dream. Trammelled with the old grave-clothes of habit, blinded by the napkin of doubt, it still hesitates and fears, till re-assured by the voice of the Lord, saying, " Loose him, and let him go." Then the world becomes a new creation, and the Divine Presence is everywhere felt. Not one's self only, but the world, has come from death into life; and the things of the world are transfigured and made holy by the perception that they are the rounds of the ladder by which we are to mount into a higher existence. The more fully the spiritual life is awakened within us, the more highly we value material life; because we see that it is the basis of the spiritual, the means by which we are to become disciplined and cultivated in the regenerating life: and, every step that we advance, we shall learn to value more and more this material apparatus with which the Creator has surrounded us; for through it, if rightly used, we shall reach to a higher and higher comprehension and appreciation of spiritual things. As this process goes on, the faith becomes more and more perceptive; gradually losing the traditional character that belonged to early life, and becoming assured with a conviction too soul-felt to admit of doubt.

There are, however, those who resist the incoming of the Spirit; who look upon faith in the supernatural experiences of the soul as superstition, regarding them as insane vagaries of the imagination; and who cling to the material with a merely sensuous love, that shuts out the spiritual.

When the Lord performed miracles upon earth, there were those who looked on, and affirmed that the power was from Beelzebub. They were told, in reply to their blasphemy, that there was one sin, the sin against the Holy Spirit, which could not be forgiven in this world or in the next.

The same lips that uttered this fearful annunciation commanded us to forgive our brother, though he sin against us seventy times seven, if he turn and repent. We must feel certain that any forgiveness of which we are capable is but the shadow of the infinite mercy of God, which is ever ready to bless the repentant sinner. A sin, then, which shuts us out from the divine forgiveness, must be one that so befools the understanding, and stupefies the affections, that it destroys the recuperative power of the soul, so that it can no longer repent.

The Lord promised that he would be with his disciples always, — even to the end of the world; and, if we are his disciples, it would seem that we should be able to recognize him, and should love to perceive him, not only in his word and works, but in our own hearts, where he reveals himself to the consciousness with an express adaptation to the individual wants of every human being, that makes the inflowing of his truth and love the most precious gift he can bestow. If we refuse to believe that he is present with us now, and shut our hearts against his coming; if we attribute the emotions he may sometimes excite in us, when we are off our guard in our opposition to him, to disorder of the body or the mind, — we must be in much the same state as those who said, " He hath a devil, and is mad : " and it would seem to be wise in us to rouse ourselves before it is too late ; before we have so pledged our being to the powers of disbelief, that we have for ever closed our spiritual perceptions.

The world of material things must vanish from our ken when the material organs of sense are closed in death ; and can we rationally hope that the spiritual senses will be found healthy and perceptive, if we have ignored spiritual things so long as we remained in the material body ? If we have measured heavenly things only by earthly standards while in the body, we have inverted the order of all things ; and our life has spread its roots deeper and deeper downward into the earth, without a corresponding growth upward towards heaven. Miserable, then, is our preparation for that eternal world towards which we are hastening, but from which we must shrink in doubt and fear, so long as our spiritual perceptions remain undeveloped.

It is a fatal delusion of the human mind, that we can love the neighbor rightly, and fulfil our social duties as we ought, without loving the Lord, and without being taught of the Holy Scriptures. No human love stands more in need of regeneration than the love we bear to ourselves; and therefore our love to the neighbor must equally need enlightenment and purification, since we are commanded to love our neighbor as ourselves. We may love the neighbor, only to pamper his vices, just as we are prone to love ourselves. Many love their children in this way; many believe that friendship requires that we love not only the virtues, but the vices, of our friend; many, that patriotism requires us to defend the doings of our country, whether right or wrong.

Love to the neighbor includes every variety of affection we may bear towards our fellow-beings, whether individually or collectively; and, in order that we may love the neighbor rightly, we must have wise views of human nature in all its various domestic, social, and civil relations. We may do as much mischief by indiscriminate indulgence towards those with whom we are brought into contact as by indiscriminate hatred.

The dealings of the Divine Providence with humanity must be a perfect exemplification of love to the neighbor. The heavenly Father is the only being capable of perfect love, — of love that ever seeks to bless, and that looks to the eternal good of humanity in all its benefactions. It gives and it takes away, it indulges and it denies, governed always by infinite mercy and infinite wisdom; and those who truly love the Lord find always a blessing hidden within his dispensations, whether they come with smiles or tears, with gifts or with bereavements.

If we would love our neighbor and ourselves aright, we must seek for wisdom to do so in the Divine Providence. Love of approbation may lead us to do much for our neighbor that can do him nothing but harm. Indolence may make us indiscriminately liberal and indiscriminately mischievous by our liberality. The dread of tears or of sad faces may make us indulgent to the caprices and whims, and even vices, of children and of friends. The east is not farther from the west than all this from any resemblance to the love the heavenly Father shows towards his children. All this is but the fruit of a hidden love of self, and contains nothing of the wisdom and mercy of that Being who seeks always the best good of his children.

The love of self, of one's own qualities and opinions; the desire to gratify one's own tastes or passions merely because they are one's own, without regard to right or wrong, — is the natural tendency of humanity. While we are in a merely natural state, the love we bear to other persons will be of the same quality as that which we feel for ourselves. We shall be capricious, partial, prejudiced, and unjust. We may love some persons, and indeed whole classes of persons, with the most zealous ardor; but our affections will be confined within narrow limits, and we shall be liable to hate those who are without our limits as ardently as we love those who are within them. In opposition to St. Paul's noble exposition of charity, we shall not suffer long, and be kind; we shall vaunt ourselves, and be puffed up; we shall behave ourselves unseemly, seek our own, shall be easily provoked, and shall think much evil.

When the love of self becomes regenerated, we shall seek to subdue our passions and opinions to the law of right, — to the absolute truth as it is in Jesus; and then our hearts will warm towards our fellow-beings with a love that hopeth all things. Humbled by a sense of our own imperfections, we shall not be in haste to condemn others, but shall forgive as we hope to be forgiven. Not that we shall be lenient towards vice, either in ourselves or others; but that, feeling how much we stand in need of the divine mercy, we shall, in turn, be compassionate towards our fellow-sinners. Because we do not happen to sin in just the same way that they do, we shall not forget that we may be sinning in some way that is quite as offensive to our heavenly Father. The pride that exults in supposed sinlessness may sink us below the wretch, who, in presenting himself before the Lord, can only say in true humiliation of heart, "Be merciful to me, a sinner!"

The young man who had kept all the commandments from his youth, who was pre-eminently rich in good works, drew from the Lord the exclamation, "How hardly shall they that have riches enter into the kingdom of God!" It is evident that the riches of good works were here intended; because, if the Lord had spoken merely of material wealth, the disciples would hardly have been astonished, and have asked, "Who, then, can be saved?" Wandering in poverty with their divine Master, it would have pleased rather than have surprised them to be told that it was so hard for the rich to enter the heavenly kingdom. They would have exulted in the idea that the few rich were to be abased, and the many poor exalted.

When they say, "Lo, we have left all, and have followed thee!" the Lord answers again in purely figurative words, when he tells them that those who have forsaken property and friends for his sake and the gospel's, shall receive *now, in this time*, a hundred-fold, with persecutions; and in the world to come, eternal life. It is evident that persecutions could not accompany the enjoyment of so much worldly wealth: but if we put for the houses they had left the natural man which they were striving to cast from them; and for the parents, the seeming goods and truths from which their natural characters sprang; and for children, the seemingly good and true ideas and thoughts and aspirations which were the offspring of their minds while in a natural state,—we can then see, that if the disciples really cast off and left all these, and were sincerely converted from them, they would receive in their place all manner of corresponding spiritual blessings. The possession of these must bring persecution, because it would separate them from the Jewish world around them; but, in the world to come, it would insure them eternal life.

Spiritual pride, the pride that trusts in its own wealth of good works, is a sin, we are thus taught, which makes salvation almost impossible; and this is because it renders us incapable of keeping the second commandment.

As sinning against the Holy Spirit poisons the fountains of our faith, making it impossible for us to be pious towards God; so sinning against our fellow-beings in the pride that loves to say in heart, if not in word, "I am holier than thou," makes it impossible for us to be charitable towards the neighbor. The one sin is born of the pride of intellect; the other, of the pride of life. They naturally belong together, and mutually strengthen each other. We may live bond-slaves to their power, and yet lead lives of the most perfect respectability, and die lamented and eulogized by society. These two sins which the Lord denounced so fearfully, declaring that the one made salvation impossible, and the other almost so, are perfectly compatible with a life that shall make us loved and admired in our relations with the world. This makes them doubly dangerous; for it is very hard to believe that God condemns us, when the tongue of man gives us so much praise. The world loves its own; and, if the world loves us very much, it should put us on our guard, lest peradventure it so love us because we so love it.

The viper is not more insidious in its movements, or more deadly in its poison, than the love of the world within the heart, when we fail to recognize it, and to put ourselves on our guard against its devices.

A truly religious faith and life can be founded only upon the two great commandments; the first being the essence, the second the form, of all that we believe and love and do. Only so far as we comprehend and appreciate and love the Lord our God can we love the neighbor without selfishness, and understand our duty towards him. Only so far as we look to the Lord for light, and lean upon him for strength, can we embody our love to the neighbor into our lives, without danger of harming rather than helping him.

It is in seeking our own life, striving to live out our own wilfulness, that we are bewildered, if not lost, in spiritual death : but in giving up our own will, laying down our own life that we may receive the life of the Lord and do his will, we find that eternal life which we all hope for; that heavenly peace which is in the heart of every true disciple; that perfect freedom which is embodied in the harmonious life of heaven, which ever becomes more perfect as it becomes more full, because each individual loves and seeks the happiness of the whole.

While listening to the voices of many individuals talking at the same time in a social party, every one has been struck by the discordance of the sound. This discord represents the want of harmony in the hearts of those thus met together; for the tone of the voice corresponds to the affections of the soul. This sound is the result of that freedom which man loves in his unregenerate state, — the freedom to do as he pleases, without regard to God or the neighbor.

Every one has listened with delight to the exquisite cadences of sound produced by the wind in a wood, especially among pine-trees, or by the waves rolling in upon a beach. Myriads of leaves or of drops of water combine to produce these two great choirs of the material world; and yet the result is the most delicious harmony. The reason of this is, that each leaf and each wave moves in exact obedience to the laws of gravitation, which, in the material world, hold all things in their true places, just as the laws of divine goodness hold all things in their true places in the spiritual world. As, in the material world around us, all discordant sounds are the result of the temporary interruption of the laws of gravitation; so, in the spiritual world within us, all discordance is caused by our disobedience to the laws of the Divine Goodness. The discordant sounds of nature typify the selfish liberty which we enjoy when regardless of the laws of love to God and the neighbor: the harmonious sounds typify the heavenly freedom which we love when we seek to do what is right because it is God's law. We are slow to perceive the beauty of this freedom, and, at first, it looks to us like bondage; but, so soon as we begin to come into it, we feel that not to love it would be like loving to sing and play out of time and tune. No one, who has any ear for music, would feel it a desirable state of freedom to be a discordant unit in an orchestra or choir: on the contrary, it would be a bondage that could give only pain and annoyance. So the discord which comes of the want of piety and morality affects the spiritual sense of the regenerate soul with the keenest anguish: while the concord which results from obedience to the laws of the divine harmony affords a delight as far beyond that which results from any earthly music, as the spiritual transcends the material; the infinite, the finite; the eternal, that which endures but for a day.

THE PAST AND THE FUTURE.

The past and the future exist as one in the present; for the present is at once the fruit of the past, and the seed of the future.

THE PAST AND THE FUTURE.

FEW minds are entirely absorbed in the present hour. The past, with its store of memories, pleasant or painful, still clings to us; and the future, with its multifarious hopes and fears, occupies a large proportion of our thoughts.

We are apt to think too little of our thoughts, and to let them take their own course too freely, without considering that they are capable of every degree of good or evil, no less than our words or our actions. "Vain regrets, and hopes as vain," too often enervate our powers, and unfit us for the proper performance of the duties of life that belong to the present day; making life a sorrow and a care, instead of a daily offering of submission and trust.

Rightly to acquiesce in the past, and rightly to anticipate the future, are Christian duties too much neglected; by many scarcely placed among duties, or perhaps even quite forgotten.

We are prone, in our sorrowful and our anxious moods of mind, to magnify our own powers and our own accountabilities, and not to think enough of the Omnipotence that "shapes our ends, rough-hew them how we will." We surround the past with a cloud of "ifs" wherewith to imbitter memory. If we had done this, or if we had not done that, something we can never cease to regret might never have happened: and yet, perhaps, the act done or omitted was one whose bearings we did not at all comprehend at the time; and it could not, therefore, have been one over which we ought to grieve with any feeling of remorse. So, too, in regard to events over which we ourselves had no control, we often feel, that if others had done their duty, or if some event had only fallen out a little differently from what it did, all might have been as we could wish. Our fortune might not have been lost, our friend might not have died, our hopes might not have been disappointed; in short, we might have had our own way, and not have been obliged to bear the cross allotted to us. We forget that our heavenly Father was there, and could easily have overruled all these mistakes, or permitted all these " ifs," had it seemed best to his wisdom; and therefore the event demands our humble acquiescence; and it is resisting the will of the heavenly Father if we refuse to be comforted, or if we fail to acknowledge his presence and his power in what has come to pass. "If thou hadst been here, our brother had not died!" was the exclamation of the unbelieving sisters as they met the Lord, who had waited for the death of Lazarus that he might the more wonderfully show forth his power; and this is the exclamation of every heart that gives way to unavailing regret for the past. It does not believe that the Lord was near when the sorrowful event took place. It exalts the human above the divine in the affairs of life, and cannot believe that there is a special Providence caring for its welfare, more constantly, more wisely, and more mercifully, than it can care for itself.

So in regard to the future: while we should take every wise precaution in order to insure success to our plans and anticipations, we should be careful to remember that the Lord is always supreme, and that in his hands are the issues of our lives.

Circumstances are never entirely in our power; but it is in our power to make a good use even of the worst in the training of our own minds and hearts. We should watch the workings of our thoughts and affections, and see whether good or evil is developed in them by the daily events of our lives; whether we are patient and long-suffering and kind, when our plans are frustrated and our hopes are disappointed; or whether we are offended and inconsolable, discontented with ourselves and with Providence.

Most persons live more in the future than the present. Our now is seldom so satisfactory that we are not hoping for something better to come. But whether the future will be any better or happier than the past or the present, depends much more upon the culture we bestow upon ourselves than on the care we take for the circumstances that surround us. When the disciples were looking forward for a future, external kingdom of heaven, the Lord told them that it was within themselves; and, in the same way, each of us carries about a kingdom of happiness or of misery within his own heart, created by his own affections, and only in some measure modified by surrounding circumstances. Therefore the more we regard the future of our mental and moral development, and the less we think about the future of external life, the better and happier we shall become.

The future that we hope for is the index of our mental state; and, if we desire to know ourselves, we can probably do so in no more ready way than by observing our hopes and wishes as they rise spontaneously in our minds.

We wish lazily for many things without ever going in pursuit of them. We fancy that we really wish to possess them; but still we never set ourselves diligently to obtain them. An examination of these wishes would show us the negative side of our characters. There are other things that we wish for eagerly, that we pursue with ardor, that we strive for with all our might; and these wishes reveal the positive side of the character.

These words *negative* and *positive* are not used in an exact and philosophic sense in this connection: but they may serve to designate, on the one hand, those desires or impulses of the mind which have an actual existence, but are controlled and neutralized by others; and, on the other hand, those which are powerful and victorious, and come forth into the life.

In society, we often hear persons exclaiming, "How I wish I could do this or that!" "How I wish I possessed this or that accomplishment!" "How I wish I were good-tempered, like this one! or industrious and persevering, like that one!" The larger number of these wishes are uttered in a tone which plainly indicates that there is no vitality in the wish; that the speaker has no intention of trying to obtain the thing wished for; that the words in which it was uttered came from the tongue only, and not from the heart. These are all negative wishes. The wisher did not desire the accomplishments or virtues he talked of, so much because he loved them, as because he saw that they made their possessor admired in society; or perhaps he thought that those to whom he spoke would feel some degree of admiration for him, merely because he expressed a desire for that which was esteemed admirable in others; or perhaps it soothed his own vanity, to believe, for the moment, that he really desired to become better or wiser than he felt himself to be. Other wishes we hear spoken in an earnest tone, as if they came out from the abundance of the heart; and we feel assured that the speaker will at once set about attaining the object wished for. These are positive wishes, and will result in effort; and in proportion as they are vital, and truly belong to the character, they will be obtained.

If we look within our own hearts, we shall find a little world there, going on in a mode similar to that of the larger world of society in which we live. Each one of us has his negative and his positive wishes; is pleasing himself with believing that he is the better for forming wishes that he never ultimates in action, because they are negative wishes; or wishing from his heart for things that he will obtain, because he wishes for them positively.

The mind tends naturally to estimate itself by its negative rather than by its positive traits; by the things which it desires passively, rather than by the things which it desires actively. The things which we desire passively, we desire with the thoughts of the understanding; while the things which we desire actively, we desire with the affections of the heart. We incline to estimate ourselves by our thoughts, rather than by our affections; because the understanding can measure the thoughts with ease, while the affections are too secret and too interior to be sounded by any line that the understanding can cast.

The impulses of active life come from the hidden sources of the affections, while the thoughts serve only as guides and helps to ultimate the affections in the outward life. The understanding is thus the servant of the will or heart, and is neither so good nor so evil as its master. The thoughts desire what the understanding tells them is wise, while the affections desire what the heart tells them is good. The understanding gives its reasons for the faith that is in it, in clear and precise words, making every thing palpable and distinct in the thoughts; and, as we reason within ourselves, we believe that these wise thoughts are our very selves. The reasonings of the heart or will are intuitive, and far quicker than those of the understanding: so quick, that the understanding cannot take cognizance of them as they are formed; and so interior, that it never entirely comprehends them. The understanding gives life to the perceptions and thoughts: the will gives life to the affections, emotions, and passions.

Much of what passes in the world for hypocrisy is the result of a want of harmony between the understanding and the will. Men talk morally and wisely about ethics and religion, because they are sensible; and then go away and act foolishly and wickedly, because they have selfish and evil hearts.

Peter was perfectly sincere when he told the Lord he would die rather than deny him; but the selfishness of his will overcame him at the first temptation. What is sinful is always foolish; and, as we think about sin in the abstract, its folly compels our understanding to condemn it: but presently the choice is brought directly home to us, whether to commit this sin, or to deny ourselves, and perhaps to take up a heavy cross; and our hearts, as it were, die within us, and we sin, perhaps impulsively, like Peter; perhaps delibeately, like Iscariot.

It is a common mistake in education to suppose, that, if the intellectual faculties are thoroughly trained, evil will be crowded out of the mind by the force of rationality. Unfortunately, although rationality teaches us the folly of all evil things in the abstract, and makes us see how foolish they are in other people, it does very little, if any thing, towards opening our eyes to our own follies; or, if it compel us to acknowledge them to be follies, it by no means follows that it prevents us from committing them, because our dominant wishes are very sure to be stronger than our rationality.

It has been well remarked by a writer on education, that "it is the *wish* of the young mind which first trains the faculties." What the child wishes for, generally decides what the man will wish for. The chief end of education should be to lead the child to desire what is truly good from good motives; and the chief end of self-training should be to learn what is intrinsically good, and then to seek after it, with singleness of heart, because it is good.

Whatever we love seems good to us, so long as we are in a natural or unregenerate state. The first movement we make towards a spiritual or regenerate state, we discover that there is an absolute good; a something that is good, though we may not love it. We can have an intellectual perception of this absolute good, long before we learn to love it, and possibly without ever learning to love it at all. We acknowledge in our own minds that we are possessed by evil habits and passions, and we determine to break away from them, and rise above them; but, when the hour of temptation comes, we fall again and again, even when we finally escape from the bondage of sin. Too often, however, we go on to the end of our temporal lives, slaves to sins, the evil of which we recognize intellectually, with perfect distinctness, but which we never abandon, because our affections have never come into agreement with our intelligence.

One of the great dangers of life is the deception we are liable to fall into, of believing that we truly wish to be possessed of some particular virtue, while we are continually falling into the opposite vice. No one can do this, unless he really loves the vice, and wishes for its enjoyment. When not assailed by temptation, our intelligence shows us the evil consequences of our vices; and then the dread of those consequences causes us to determine that we will avoid them in future by ceasing to sin : but, the moment temptation comes, the wish for indulgence is aroused, and we fall. This is because our wish for the vice is positive, while the wish for the opposite virtue is negative. The positive can be expelled from the soul, only by the positive. We may think that we have cast a sin out of doors for ever, and complacently sweep and garnish the vacant house : but, while it is vacant, there is nothing to hinder the return of the old tenant, or to prevent his bringing seven other sins with him, whenever the hour of temptation opens the door; and, each time that this happens, the soul falls into a lower state than before. Here was no conversion. The wish of the heart remained, all the time, the same. It was stunned, for a while, by the blow the understanding gave it, when it cast it out of doors; but by the time the understanding, supposing its work finished, began to think about something else, the old wish was all alive again, and ready to return to its former abode. The difficulty of driving vice out of the heart, in this way, is not great; but there is nothing harder than to keep it out ever afterwards. To do this, a positive virtue must take the place where the old vice dwelt. Then there is a true conversion, a genuine regeneration of the heart. The wish is "born again," and, from positive evil, is become positive good.

We are told by the Lord, "No man can come to me, except the Father draw him." That is, no man can come to the truth, unless he is drawn to it by goodness. No man can love the truth as it is in God the Son, unless he loves goodness as it is in God the Father.

No one who is not fatuous with vice can read the moral code revealed by the Lord, and hesitate to acknowledge that obedience to it would make earth heaven. But, alas! no one can read it, and not feel that his heart rebels against it somewhere. There is no one who does not wish for something that the Lord tells him he must not have, and must not desire; no one who in all things loves his neighbor as himself, and the Lord above all. The despairing soul inquires with trembling, "Who, then, can be saved?" and the answer comes, "The things which are impossible with men are possible with God." Our own unregenerate understandings may cast vice out from the soul for a little while; but God only can give us a virtue to fill the vacant place, and thereby make the return of vice impossible. If we have ever effectually cast out a vice without going to our heavenly Father for the power, and in all humility acknowledging that the power is his alone, we have filled the vacant room with some other vice stronger than the one we cast out, and our last state is worse than our first. Pride is a demon, mighty for this work. It tells us to avoid vice, that we may be respectable, that we may be rich, that we may rise to high places, that we may look down upon our neighbors; and it can swell itself so largely as to fill every one of the vacant rooms our other vices have occupied. It is the father of a legion of other vices, and, like Saturn, devours its children, that they may not dethrone him. If any doubt that this is so, let him ask himself, "When I am under the dominion of pride, to whom do my wishes tend?" and the only answer he can make is, "To mine own self." There is no worship of God in pride, and there is no love for the neighbor. To the proud man, self is the only God; and the neighbor is valued, only as he helps to glorify self.

We are told by the Lord, "No man cometh unto the Father but by me;" and again, "I am the way." There is no contradiction between these assertions and that previously quoted, "No man can come unto me, except the Father draw him." These truths sustain and are essential to each other. We cannot love the truth, unless we love goodness; but, again, we can only learn to love goodness by doing the truth. We cannot come unto the Son, unless the Father draw us; that is, we cannot arrive at the truth, unless we are drawn to it by the love of goodness: and we cannot come unto the Father but through the Son; that is, we can arrive at goodness, only by walking in the way of truth, by obeying the words of the Son, who was himself the Word of God.

There are three degrees of life in the will, — affection, emotion, and passion; and these three severally express themselves in wishes, aspirations, and prayers. We first wish for a thing, then aspire after it, then pray for it. If the will tend only towards self and the world, our wishes, aspirations, and prayers will be directed in a way that will drag us continually downward in the scale of being. This is sometimes the case with persons who take an intellectual pleasure in contemplating the law of the Lord, and who therefore fancy themselves religious, but who love religion only as a speculation of the understanding, and never apply it to their lives. Let such persons watch the movements of their own minds, and they will find that their wishes are limited by self and the world; that their aspirations tend only to the things of the world; that their prayers even do not take hold upon the things of heaven, and, if verbally proffered in the name of the Lord, are really uttered only in the name of self.

If the will be filled with love to God and the neighbor, its affections, emotions, and passions are all instinct with heavenly fire; and as they warm into wishes, glow in aspirations, or burn in prayer, all things are desired, sought after, and prayed for, with a view to heavenly use. Then we seek the Father through obedience to the Son; and the Father draws us, so that obedience to the Son becomes possible.

The aspirations and prayers of the human beings who surround us are known with certainty only to the Omniscient Mind. We can judge of them, only as they ultimate themselves through wishes in the material world; for we fashion the world around us in accordance with our wishes. Every human dwelling-place is compacted of the wishes of its inmates. Every human character is the embodiment of the wishes of the individual mind. The wishes of the mind train the faculties, both of head and heart, all through life. Save in those few exceptional cases where bodily infirmity or the pressure of outward circumstances prohibits freedom of action, it is the wish of the mind that determines whether the body shall dwell amid squalid poverty or thrifty comfort. It is the wish of the mind that decides whether the intellect shall abide in ignorance and weakness, or be nourished and made strong by education. It is the wish of the mind that makes the heart harder and more callous every day, or grow in grace continually; and, when the gates of death are passed, it is still the wish of the mind that gives the final answer, whether the immortal spirit shall sink into hell, or rise to heaven.

Wishes may ultimate themselves in wealth, in education, in high position, whether the aspirations and prayers of the mind tend earthward or heavenward; for the possessions of this life are in themselves neither good nor evil, but derive their quality from the motives for which they are sought, and the purposes to which they are applied. During the early periods of life, the two classes, of those who look up and those who look down, are often difficult to distinguish. As life advances, the growth of character begins to show the more secret tendencies of the soul; and old age, at last, rarely fails to exhibit the full development of the principles, whether good or evil, that were adopted in youth.

It is not uncommon to hear avarice, selfishness, ill-temper, and other vices, excused on the plea that the perpetrator is old; as if it were to be expected that we should shed our virtues as we do our hair and our teeth. If the soul died with the body, such an excuse might be rational, because then it would naturally become weak and decrepit as the strength of the body failed; but, since the soul casts off the body in order that it may rise into a higher life, if its wishes and hopes tend toward that life, the soul would become more full of heavenly traits with every added year.

The good man and the bad man often wish for the same thing; but one wishes from a bad motive, and the other from a good one. If we would lead heavenly lives, we must not only wish for good things, but must wish for them from good motives. We must watch our wishes as they form themselves, and often stop in our course to ask ourselves why we are wishing for that which we pursue. They who wish for good things from good motives will never grow into an old age that shall be less lovely than their youth; for each year must add new graces to their characters, as it brings them nearer to their heavenly home.

There is a fearful downward tendency in the human soul. The thrifty, active laborer too often becomes, in later life, the churlish miser; the frugal, industrious housewife sinks into the shrewish, hard old woman; the careful, energetic merchant becomes narrow and avaricious; the politician, a mere man of expedients; the fine woman of society, as the period of her sway passes by, grows discontented, overbearing, and fault-finding. Wherever we look, throughout society, sad examples abound, that if we look at them aright, in a spirit of humility, and not of pride, will teach us to avoid the dangers that have proved fatal to so many who have gone before us.

There is no time when humility is more needful than when we are contemplating the vices of our fellow-beings; for we are never so liable to sin ourselves as when we are looking, in a spirit of self-gratulation, at the sins of others. Pride goes before a fall, because it puts us off our guard, and blinds us to the fact that we also are weak, and liable to sin, if not in the same way as those about us, in some other way just as bad. The sins of our neighbor should awaken our sympathy and compassion, and so make us willing and able to aid him in turning away from his sin; which we can never do, if we meet him in a spirit of pride: and, at the same time, it should arouse our watchfulness in regard to our own liability to wrong-doing, and make us pray more earnestly, "Lead us not into temptation."

We are commanded to watch and to pray; and the watching is quite as needful as the prayer. We pray to the Lord, and we watch ourselves; and the watching is the reciprocal action of the prayer. The moment watchfulness ceases, prayer becomes a negative action of the mind. It is to no purpose that the sentinel remains at his post, if his eyes are closed in sleep. While we are young in religious life, it is natural for us to be on our guard; but, so soon as we begin to feel any thing like security in our position, we begin to diminish our watchfulness. Then our prayers lose their fervor, our aspirations their warmth, and our wishes become bounded by the love of self and of the world. The Christian life is a continual warfare with self-love and worldliness; and, whatever form these assume, we must challenge them, and compel them to confession. Our daily life is a perpetual succession of wishes. The pulsations of the heart send not the blood with a more steady flow through the arteries, than the affections of the will send forth their wishes through the soul. As these are pure or impure, selfish or charitable, heavenly or earthly, the spiritual life becomes angelic or infernal. As we value our eternal lives, we must watch this long file of wishes as they rise, and question them whence they come, and whither they would go; and we must be satisfied only with the plainest and fullest answers. It will not do to imagine that some are good, and some are bad; and that, if the majority are good, we are safe. As the character becomes fixed, they gradually take their position all on one side or the other. It is only while the character is forming, that the good and the bad, as it were, balance each other. When it becomes formed, the wishes all tend one way. We may sometimes stumble, or even fall, in our course, from the weakness of the flesh or of the spirit; but our wishes all tend towards the heavenly city, if we watch and pray with faithful hearts. The soldier of Christ cannot serve two masters; and if, in an unguarded moment, he becomes entangled with the soldiers of Mammon, he will soon find his mistake, and flee from the ways of temptation. He may, from weakness, sometimes be overcome; but he is never found wilfully fighting on the wrong side. Humanity is imperfect, even in the best of Christians, and no one can cease entirely from sin; but let us never forget, that, so long as we indulge ourselves wilfully and habitually in the practice of one sin, we are traitors to the cause we pretend to serve.

An habitual watchfulness over our wishes as they rise, allowing none to go forth into act but such as we can pray may be blessed of Heaven, and an habitual acknowledgment that it is only as we open our hearts to receive the heavenly blessing that we are capable of leading a heavenly life, must constitute our only safety. Watchfulness gives the shield of purity, and prayer gives the sword of strength; and, thus armed and protected, the battle is sure to be ours.

The past gives us wisdom, if we remember it rightly; the present gives us opportunity for bringing our wisdom forth into life; and our whole future will be the result and embodiment of past and present. We must not look forward to the future as to something quite apart from the past and the present; for to-morrow is now building up out of yesterday and to-day. Time is one long chain, however numerous its links; and our life is all bound up in a unity that cannot be separated. The present is a perpetual resurrection of the past; and the future exists only in imagination, until it ceases to be future, and becomes present. To-day is all that we can, in any measure, control; and, so far as we make each to-day faithful in duty, we shall look back upon the past without regret, and forward to the future without anxiety or fear.

WAR AND PEACE.

Truth is many-sided, and our limited vision can grasp it only in parts: thus we are often led to doubt its being truth, because the parts we are able to see at one time do not make a harmonious whole.

WAR AND PEACE.

WAR seems to many minds to be the natural state of the earth, and all that it contains. The elements are perpetually at strife. Winds and waves; electricity and magnetism; earth shaken by internal convulsion, or disintegrated by the action of air and water; chemical and mechanical power acting upon both the mineral and vegetable world,—all are working to destroy present forms, as if creation were for no other end than destruction.

The animal world offers a similar picture. From the minutest insect discovered by the microscope, to the hugest of beasts and fishes, all are at war, offensively or defensively; all are either devouring or devoured.

Man again repeats the same story. Whether savage or civilized, ever the strong is striving to destroy the weak, ever the fierce is tyrannizing over the timid.

Side by side with all this destruction, the peaceful power of creation goes on as constantly, re-constructing, re-organizing, revivifying the world; silently but steadily working with a power strong enough to overrule destruction, and bring a new order, better than that which went before, out of what seemed the defeat of all system or plan.

The changes of day and night and of the seasons of the year offer a very perfect type of the greater cycles of the world. To him who should first see the setting sun, knowing nothing of the certainty of its re-appearance, how fearful would be the coming-down of the evening darkness! how terrible the weary hours of night! And winter, coming like an overpowering army and conquering the face of the earth, to one who had never seen its progress and its passing-away, would seem like the veritable death of the world. In due time, darkness yields to light; and the cold of winter yields to the peaceful warmth of spring-time, and is more than conquered by the creative heat of summer.

So order came out from chaos; so creation ever follows destruction; so life wakes up from death;

so beauty rises out from ashes, and mourning is exchanged for the oil of joy.

The order of nature is found in all things to be progress through alternations of defeat and success. There is no such thing as steady, prosperous growth. All things have their intervals of pause, decline, or even retrograde movement, however successful they may be finally. Final success to all things that should prevail is certain as day is sure to follow night, or summer to take the place of winter.

In our haste, we are often tempted to think that Providence is not on the side of right; that injustice is more powerful than justice, vice than virtue; and that the progress of the world is downward to final destruction. Yet an enlightened view of any prolonged, historic period shows us, that, as centuries have rolled by, mankind have made great advances in rightful development, though their feet have often staggered in carnage, and their eyes been blinded by what seemed blackest night of falsehood.

The peace-giving, creative power is stronger than the contentious, destructive power. The love of God is omnipotent, and must finally prevail. Slowly but surely, order and harmony and peace march onward with silent tread, subduing all things to his gracious purposes. The doubter asks: Why this slowness, if the power of peace be omnipotent? Because man is endowed with free will, and the Divine Wisdom seeks to draw him to goodness, without infringing upon his liberty. The Creator might have endowed man with all good attributes, so that he should be faithful to them as animals are to their instincts; but then man would have been only a higher animal, whereas the Creator desired him to be a voluntary human being, free to choose between good and evil.

The world in which he is placed, imperfect as himself, yet full of capacities whereby it may approach perfection, is designed to instruct him by types and figures as to what he is, and to what he may attain. The Scriptures, in a more distinct and perfect, yet still typical language, give him the same instruction; and to them he must look for his highest enlightenment.

In the Scriptures, we find what at first seems contradiction, in the warlike. threatenings and peaceful promises that alternate through its pages. Creation and destruction, in the works of God, are parallel with peace and war in his Word.

The omnipotent Father permits destruction and war, that the evil may be subdued, and give place to the good. He is at once the God of battles and the Prince of peace. He makes bare his arm to smite the wicked, and keeps those in perfect peace who stay their souls on him.

At the birth of the Lord Jesus Christ, he was announced by angelic choirs as one who should bring "peace on earth, and good-will toward men." Before parting with his disciples, he said to them, "Peace I leave with you, my peace I give unto you; not as the world giveth give I unto you." After performing his miracles of healing upon the suffering, his usual salutation was, "Go in peace." On the other hand, he says, "Think not that I am come to send peace on earth: I came not to send peace, but a sword. For I am come to set a man at variance against his father, and the daughter against her mother, and the daughter-in-law against her mother-in-law; and a man's foes shall be they of his own household."

The letter killeth, but the spirit giveth life. Man attains to peace by and through war, whether we consider him individually or collectively. Each man and woman, who wins salvation, wins it through war, and so comes into that peace which passeth all understanding. In a similar way, nations, through war and all its tribulations, are brought, century by century, something nearer the kingdom of heaven.

In the heart of each one of us, there is a household corresponding to that which is about us in the external world. The ruling intellectual principle within us corresponds to our father; and the ruling affection, to our mother. Below these are subordinate principles and affections, which are as brothers and sisters to us; and, again, there are other principles and affections developed in our minds, which are as sons and daughters. All these must be regenerated before we can come into a state of peace. The being born again is not a thing of generalities, but of particulars and of details. All the principles and affections must be changed from natural to spiritual, from earthly to heavenly, before we can form a peaceful household.

It is no easy or peaceful task to bring all the members of this household into subjection to the laws of truth and goodness. There will be wars, and rumors of war, so long as pride, ambition, worldliness, vanity, envy, discontent, anger, censoriousness, and all the other hydra-like heads of our unregenerate nature, with more or less strength and endurance, assert their claims for indulgence. The catalogue of vices looks very ugly, and we are fain to believe that it does not belong to us; but who among us is without sin? Whose heart has no secret evils, hidden though they may be from others by prudence, good breeding, or other masks, that our desire for the good opinion of our neighbors helps us to put on? Not until we can abstain from all wrong, whether of deed or word or thought, because we love the Lord and our neighbor, is our warfare over, and our peace attained.

Still, there are persons who seem to others to be at peace, and who believe themselves in peace; and yet they have not gone through the warfare needful to this change. They are happy as they are, and do not see the necessity of all this effort and contention.

There are two kinds of peace, — the peace which belongs to this world, and the peace which belongs to heaven. The Lord says, "Peace I leave with you, my peace I give unto you; not as the world giveth give I unto you." Again he says, "If ye were of the world, the world would love his own; but because ye are not of the world, but I have chosen you out of the world, therefore the world hateth you."

There is a peace felt by those who love the world, and whom the world loves in return, that is very agreeable to the natural mind, and which often seems like genuine, heavenly peace. It is full of self-complacency and satisfaction. With some, it is condescending and benevolent; with others, it is ostentatious and patronizing. This is the peace which incites the prayer, "I thank thee that I am not as other men." In this peace, there is nothing that tends in any way towards spiritual growth or life; but, on the contrary, it belongs entirely to this world, and seeks only what this world can give. It glories only in its own possessions and attainments, its own kingdom and power, without giving any glory to Him from whom cometh every good and perfect gift. It values others in proportion as they minister in some way to its own dignity or pleasure; and, if it ministers to others, it is always with a desire, more or less hidden, that they, in turn, may minister to it.

Such peace makes the possessor dearly love life in this world; and many of this class would be willing to live here indefinitely, or to repeat life over again just as it has been already lived by them. There is in this peace nothing that looks toward a future life. It is all centred in the enjoyment of that which now is.

The world admires, and sometimes dearly loves, these peaceful persons; for they spend their lives in seeking the admiration and the love of the world. Verily, they receive their reward.

The peace given by the Lord to his disciples is something entirely apart from all this. His kingdom is not of this world, and his followers look constantly through this world to that which lies beyond. They seek a heavenly country while living, and through living in this. The admiration of the world gives them no satisfaction, unless their own hearts tell them that their Master says, "Well done, good and faithful servants!" Then they feel that they can enter into the joy of their Lord. Their peace is the only true liberty; for, through it, they are made independent of the world and of their own passions.

Such peace is not easily attained. It is reached through steadfast combat with the legion of wrong thoughts, affections, and propensities, that infest the human heart. It can be found only through self-denial, tribulation, and warfare: but, for this treasure, we may rejoice to sell all that we have beside; no matter how much the world may admire it, or admire us for holding it in possession.

Nations, like individuals, go through all these states of contention and warfare in the progressive growth of the ages; and they have their states of worldly peace also, between their periods of warfare. National peace and prosperity do not necessarily imply a state of national health; for they may have, as in the individual, only pride and worldliness for their foundation. Immense wealth, and progress in the arts that tend to make life convenient and elegant, often precede great national calamity.

Nations, no less than individuals, must learn their lessons of humility through disappointment, fear, and tribulation. National success induces pride and arrogance, a love of conquest, and the desire of rule. These passions make nation rise up against nation, and have induced all the wars that have desolated the earth.

Nations commit great crimes, and fancy that their strength insures them from punishment; but a day of reckoning is sure to come, though it may be long delayed.

Our heavenly Father is very patient. He waits as if wishing to offer every possible opportunity for the sinner to repent and reform; but at length the punishment comes as a natural result and consequence of the sin, and the might that knows no right but its own selfish will is humbled at the feet of its victim.

Civil wars have always been more obstinate and malignant than wars carried on by different nations, as family quarrels are most difficult to reconcile; and contentions waged within our own hearts are those that cause us the keenest anguish. Where we feel as though we had most right to expect friendliness and peace, we are most deeply and angrily disappointed if our expectations are not satisfied.

It is very difficult, while the punishment of our sins is upon us, to comprehend the justice, the wisdom, and the mercy of that which we are suffering. We are apt to think that mercy can be shown only by the forgiveness of our sins, and the indulgence of our wishes: but sin cannot be forgiven until it is repented of; and to stop the sinner in his course, and compel him to obedience to the laws of justice, is the truest mercy, — the mercy of the highest wisdom.

The immediate distress occasioned by war causes many persons to feel as though no peace could be so bad, that it should not be preferred to war; but peace may be far more disastrous than war, if it protects injustice and cruelty. War is demoralizing: but a false peace may be far more demoralizing, by teaching men to apologize for, and to protect, social evils that kill men's souls; which is far worse than to kill their bodies.

While there is that left in the minds of men which leads them individually to injustice and tyranny, war will never cease from the earth. The human race can never come under the rule of the Prince of peace, until each individual submits himself to the law of love, and is at peace in his own household. It is in vain that peace societies labor to prevent war by appeals to kings and governments, while the hearts of the people are full of selfishness, and of desire to possess that which belongs to others.

It is a common saying, that bodies of men have no consciences; and the want of honesty and justice exhibited by civil corporations and by national councils is sometimes astonishing. The morality, and sense of right, shown by bodies of men, represents the average rectitude of the individuals that compose those bodies. The only mode by which peace societies can advance their cause is by raising the morality of the people. Two nations wishing to be just can never go to war; and civil wars are impossible among a people that have justice in their hearts. Each one of us can convert his own soul to the gospel of peace; and, having done this, his life will be the best sermon he can preach to persuade others to believe the same gospel.

In the struggles that we carry on in our own hearts, we cannot conquer our enemies, and come into a state of peace with ourselves, until we become humble, and willing to give up that which is wrong within us, and to yield to that which is right. Sometimes, after severe internal struggle, we make a false peace with ourselves by covering over and hiding our sins, so that the world cannot see them; and, compromising with what we know to be wrong, we hold fast the sin as firmly as before, perhaps in a modified form, but still in reality the same.

So nations often make false peace with each other, resorting to subterfuges and compromises, in order to escape the miseries of war; but still holding fast to evil in such wise, that the spirit of war, if not war itself, is sure to rise again out of the dregs of the old trouble.

In the civil war now going on in our own country, we shall probably abolish the sin of slavery which has occasioned it; but, unless we abolish also the spirit of hatred and contempt for the negro which makes us unwilling to give him the rights of a citizen, our work will be but half done.

The North has joined hands with the South in prolonging this terrible wrong; and a large portion of the North shows the spirit of the slaveholder in the efforts it makes to prevent the immigration of the negro, or to avoid giving him the rights of a man if he is allowed to come within its borders. We can never expiate our sin against the slave until we do what lies within our power to make him a competent citizen of a free country.

The abolition of slavery in the South will be as great a revolution of the social state as the abolition of the order of nobles in France. The masters and mistresses of the South will cling as fondly to their peculiar institution as the old French *noblesse* did to theirs; and we at the North may, in our degree, prove ourselves possessed of an entirely similar spirit by doing what we can to hold the negro in an object position in our civil and social state.

The same spirit that animates the European nobility in its oppression of the lower classes animates the slaveholder in his oppression of the slave, and the same spirit displays itself in every one of us when we strive to domineer over others who come within the scope of our power in society or in our own families; and it is this same spirit of selfish domination that causes nations to go to war with one another, and that incites civil wars.

It is natural to humanity to love to be ministered to; and therefore it is pleasing to the unregenerate mind to feel that there is an abject, servile class of beings, either white or colored, on whom we can place our burdens while we live at ease.

We cannot suppose that society can ever exist without the distinction of rich and poor, and it is difficult to imagine a society in which the rich and the poor will not have many points of antagonism; but, the more Christianized any society becomes, the less of this antagonism there will be. If a society could be formed on earth, of individuals who were true Christians, each at peace in the household of his own heart, then all antagonism between rich and poor, high and low, wise and simple, would cease; then would be seen that which has never yet been on earth, — a nation at peace with itself. Could the earth be peopled by nations such as these, war would cease, and the Prince of peace would reign supreme.

We have little reason to suppose that such a state of the world can ever exist; but this should be the model kept within our hearts by which to form our own characters. Though perfection is not within mortal grasp, or even mortal conception, we should keep before our mind's eye the highest ideal of it that we can form, in order to attain the highest good of which we are capable. If we lower our standard of excellence to what we think we can actually attain, there is danger, that, when we have attained it, we shall stop, contented with what we have done. If, on the other hand, we aim at the highest excellence we can conceive; so fast as we approach it, our mental horizon will widen, and open out regions still beyond, leading us onward in a progress that will never end.

THE END.

www.ingramcontent.com/pod-product-compliance
Lightning Source LLC
Chambersburg PA
CBHW032158160426
43197CB00008B/973